How to be a h‿‿‿‿ ‿‿‿‿‿

Book One

for kids of all ages (and intelligent adults)

©

Publication

2023 Copyright ©

Phoenix Louisa Angela Popiolek

All rights reserved.

2023 (written in 2007)

No part of this book may be reproduced in any form by photocopying or any electronic of mechanical means, including information storage or retrieval systems, without permission first from both the
Copyright owner and the publisher of the book.
All characters are fictional.
Any similarity to any actual person is purely coincidental.

tHis bOoK bEloNgs tO...

(...wHo is CoMpletEly FaNtaStic!)

For Planet Earth
and her Children
and the Remembering of the
Divine in Every Human Heart

(No matter how B for Bonkers Life Seems)

Before this story begins, a word in your ear...
Amelia Firebrand never realised how alone she felt until the day the Universe started speaking to her.
Until then she was completely normal.
A little bit bored. A little bit lonely.
But apart from that, completely Normal.
She had hands that were good for picking things up and legs that were good for walking. She was small for her age, her clothes were way too big.
She had an afro of brown curls, with a whisp of frizzy gold.
Honey soft skin and deep soulful eyes.

It was what was inside Amelia that made her truly remarkable. Like you, she had a soul. What she didn't know was that her soul was a magic one and it was as old as the Earth.
But, Amelia Firebrand did not believe in magic.
Thankfully, Magic believed in her.

DAY ONE

MONDAY

17th December

Chapter 1

Pudding Bag Lane

Dawn. The block of high-rise flats called Chewing Gum Gutters cast a long shadow across London, the silhouette making a tomb slab on the horizon. Traffic snaked through yellow snow-sludged roads, spraying subways, billboards and swaying Christmas lights with gutter gunk.
Amelia Firebrand cried out in her sleep and jerked awake. She sat upright in bed, her Jammy Biscuit Pyjamas tangled around her. She cradled her head in her hands. 'Oh no, holy macaroni…' she gulped.
It was the same nightmare, every night. Pictures of children with greying skin and forlorn eyes floating through the city flickered in her mind. Amelia clasped two fingertips to her wrist. Her pulse fluttered like a tiny bird.
Amelia got up and looked in the mirror, tugging a splodge of gooey gum out of her wild

fuzz of curls, trying to pull them straight - but they pinged back even wilder. She blew warm breath on her numb fingers and stared out the window of her bedroom on the Seventeenth Floor. A tear pooled in Amelia's eye watching a claw toed one legged pigeon stood shivering on the window ledge. Reaching up on tippy-toe, she dangled an old sock out for the bird to nuzzle into and poured her bowl of soggy Bland Flakes out for it to eat.
Amelia closed the window and gazed at her reflection in the window pane.
L is for Lonely.
Suddenly her digital watch beeped. It was time for school. Somewhere she had to find:
a) her school satchel and
b) her ginger tom-cat, Sergeant Pepper.
Amelia tugged on her grey school jumper along with her jeans that were two sizes too big. Sergeant Pepper emerged from the half-collapsed wardrobe. He had a sleepy eye and as usual one looked straight at her, bold and bright, and the other gazed down at the carpet. Amelia smiled at him and pulled on her sparkly red trainers, she fumbled in her pocket for her homemade (and rather tatty)

brown-papered, notebook. The words scrawled on the front were hard to read.

aMeliA fIrEbrAnd'S
pOcKetT booK of RaInBoWs

Amelia didn't like being called dyslexic by her school, she couldn't even spell the word! She flicked through the notebook's curled-up pages. On each page Amelia had stuck a vintage polaroid photo of a rainbow (the only thing she loved as much as her cat). Today she chose the one she had taken one grim morning, when the rainbow's end was surprisingly close to Chewing Gum Gutters. She stroked her thumb across it feeling comforted, and thought just for a millisecond that she saw a shimmer of bright light glisten and sparkle from the notebook and accross the room.

She blinked and shrugged, disregarding it, and grabbed her skateboard out from under the bed and held it still for Sergeant Pepper to clamber onto for their walk to school. 'Time to go, Sarge.' Then, they walked via the bathroom bathtub where her pet goldfish swam happily, giving it a sprinkling of Whiffy Fishy Flakes and wheeled her cat through to the sitting room.

Gramps sat jabbing at the television channels with his poking stick. His bored expression flickered in the light of the telly. 'Gramps. It's morning. B is for Breakfast,' she said grabbing him a sachet of All Good Chicks Come In Cages, ready-to-crack, Omelette Mix. Gramps burped, took a drag on his cigarette and pushed her away - the morning snooker coverage was starting. Amelia sighed. Sergeant Pepper tugged on the skateboard, Amelia nodded and turned to leave the flat.
Her heart sank like a stone.
I is for Invisible.
Outside on the cold streets, her nose burned with the frost. Amelia eyeballed the clouds, afraid that as she felt so sad, they and the whole sky might fall in on her head. She fastened the buckle of her bright-yellow crash-hat and it reflected against her honey brown skin like a buttercup.
Amelia hopped on her bicycle and pedalled along the pavement of Pudding Bag Lane.

Sergeant Pepper's skateboard trailed behind
her from a string around her wrist. She
whizzed past the kebab shop and waved at Mr
Mincey. Then Amelia saw the Queen of England
on a billboard advertising the annual
Christmas Day Speech. It looked really boring!
Amelia liked to daydream and wondered what the
Queen would look like if she had a big fuzzy
head of curls, like Amelia or a full afro like
her mama had!
Amelia's heart sank again.
O is for Orphan.
Amelia turned her head back to looking in the
direction she was moving in. But it was too
late.
Just moments away from an exhaust fume
blackened statue of an angel - CLANG!
Amelia cycled into a London City bin.
She flew over the handlebars. Her mouth opened
to scream, but nothing came out. Time
stretched outwards in every direction in a big
yawn. Amelia had always wanted to fly. But not
like this, she thought, as the pavement zoomed
towards her at a million miles an hour.
She crash-landed on the pavement with a horrid
yowl. Her eyeballs rolled in her skull in a

wave of nausea. Without warning she welcomed her Bland Flakes back on to the paving slabs and felt her cheeks burning with shame. She pushed herself up with her grazed palms. Bruises surfaced on her forehead, her hands, her knees, her legs. Her bright-yellow-crash hat had saved her life.
Pedestrians cleared a channel around her but continued hurrying to work.
'Help!' A tiny whisper left Amelia's throat. 'Help!' She reached up with her numb hand. The bustling crowds ignored her. Their forest of coats cloaked her in a dense musty darkness. Amelia rolled into a ball on the paving slabs to save herself. Sergeant Pepper leapt from his overturned skateboard to protect her.
Tears sprung from Amelia's eyes, but for a moment her world went black. Sergeant Pepper's claws gripped though her coat making Amelia's head pound harder. Feet trampled her deeper into the sludge, closer and closer to a horrible end.
A loved and cared-for child might leap into the air and brush themselves off.

But not Amelia Firebrand. Something ached inside her. Something fearful and sad that she couldn't reach. A feeling in her that something was missing. A feeling that made her want to give up breathing.

Above her, a crystalline dew drop rolled from the eye of the face of the angel statue, landing on Amelia.

But she didn't see it.

Curled in that sludgy ball, Amelia's short life flashed before her.

Amelia Firebrand.

No friends.

No Mama.

No Papa.

Just a cat.

A skateboard.

A bicycle...

BUT! with one very BIG heart.

A big glassy bright tear rolled down her cheek and wet the pavement. The love in this tear was so alive it shone crystalline bright.

Suddenly! Without warning, the ground jolted beneath Amelia. Her body was jerked upright.

WA-WHOOM!

The ground quaked.

WA-WOMB
Amelia stared in astonishment.
Her hands were luminescent!
WA-WHOOM.
And beneath her cold knees.
There it was.
There it was again. A slow, rhythmic thud.
A heartbeat.
With a thrill of excitement, Amelia shuffled to get up realising that the earth beneath London was alive and breathing?
Amelia was not alone. She looked up to the sky, clouds parted and light shone... just for a moment, with grazed palms she felt the earth's heart beat with a comforting and gentle thud through every part of her being
WA-WHOOM
She leapt to her feet and pushed away the grown-ups. They fell back like skittles.

Amelia looked down at the frosted weeds that poked through the cracks of the concrete. She looked closer. They were reaching towards the light to grow with silvery-soft whispers. Amelia listened enchanted and pressed the soft of her fingertips to her cheeks.

Was everything ALIVE? she wondered. Even the ground beneath London… and she looked up at the sky, it seemed to be listening to her, suddenly eveything felt so alive...? Was it? Were the stars the universe above her, and the insignificant and scraggly weeds beneath her? Alive with a heartbeat, like Amelia, but with everyone too busy to notice? Too sad and busy to see?

Amelia stood on wobbly knees and shuffled with her bike and the trailing skateboard to get out of the way of the hordes of pedestrians which were streaming past her like a runny nose. She looked down at her palms, they were grazed with grit. She brushed it off, her skin rippling with a sharp sting. And through the soles of her sparkly red trainers and up softly through her feet she felt it again.

WA-WHOOM!

WA-WHOOM!

WA-WHOOM!

Amelia eyes shone bright, her feet feeling planted on the ground, she smiled up at the sky, feeling somehow an infinite big universe beyond the clouds smiling with her, her heart felt so free. She poked her fingertip to her nose and squidged her nose sideways to check if she was even really real in disbelief.

It IS real. She said. MAGIC

The world has a beating heart like me. And all of life is alive… and whispering to me?

Amelia thought maybe she was...

B for Bonkers.

She looked around at everyone trailing past in dull grey suits, and high heeled shoes and realised that, No, she and everything still looked...

N for Normal.

Or was it?

Amelia rubbed her eyes with her knuckles.

'Uh-oh!'

WA-WHOOM!

She looked around to realise and the world never looked the same again.

The entrance to London Underground's Pudding Bag Lane Tube Station billowed with a massive sneeze. Amelia rocked back on her heels. Unknown to the commuters, the entrance had sprayed them with black tube snot and had sent their hair whooshing up from their heads. Amelia gawped. Then she gawped some more.
'Sergeant Pepper, are you seeing th of a voice. Amelia gasped as a security camera swivelled on its post, an eye bulged out of it staring at them both.
Sergeant Pepper clambered up on to the dented bin, his orange fur electrified with fright.
Amelia scanned the crowd at the school gates to see if any other kids were seeing the same thing.
Instead, what she saw made her eyes pop out on stalks.
'My nightmare! The other kids, look at them!' Amelia pointed. Their skin, no matter if it was naturally black, white or brown – was draining away to a pallid GREY.

'No, no, tube stations don't sneeze! Children don't turn grey!' Amelia rubbed her bruised head. Had the earth been speaking to her in her dreams?

Perhaps she had concussion and should see a doctor? Yes. That was it.
A black cloud passed overhead. Amelia could just about pull her anorak hood up over her bright-yellow-crash-hat. The toots and honks of passing traffic seemed louder. The stink of the fumes filled her chest. She looked up at the face of the angel statue gazing into its still and calm eyes. Illumianting the grey streets, a light seemed to shimmerfrom it 'Holy ravioli, What's happening?' she said to it. 'I must be losing my marble.' The clouds thickened and started to sleet. Sergeant Pepper jumped to hide in Amelia's bicycle basket and Amelia hurried them both over and through the school gates. "Help!" Amelia cried in her squeaky soft whisper of a voice.

Chapter 2

London's School for No-Good Children

A thick wedge of snow fell from the plastic plaque splattered with pigeon plops and on to Amelia's crash-hat. 'Arrrgh,' she grimaced and locked her bike to the railings. The now, snowless plaque announced her school as... London's School for No-Good Children. Amelia grimaced and fastened her crash-hat tighter; deciding that from this day forth, she would never, ever take it off. London was clearly madder than a rollerskating-chainsaw and she didn't know what was coming next. She couldn't have known. How could she? Being so small, and ugly too, everyone told her.
It could have all been her imagination. She could have made it all up. But there was a little voice in her wondering if the Earth's heartbeating and the sky listening and the underground's sneezing might not be

M for Mad, but instead be...

M for Magic.

She could never ask her teacher, Mrs Pencil-Sharpener, no, not in a million years. Mrs Pencil-Sharpener would only send her to detention. She couldn't speak to Gramps; because, well... it was Gramps and he never wanted her to bother him. Ever.

Amelia looked up surprised. From a bush in the playground, right there in front of her, a TV presenter appeared! He stepped out of the bush wearing what looked like, his granny's knitted jumper. A large orange butterfly was embroidered on its front. Amelia held on to Sergeant Pepper feeling his soft purr. Amelia recognised the man.

'It's that one off the telly with woolly jumpers and a beard the size of a candyfloss,' she whispered, making herself as small as she possibly could. 'The one off nature programmes!' She watched him with curiosity as he crept through the crowds of children in the playground as though he were on a safari jungle adventure. But! Not one of them blinked! Amelia realised. She must be the only one who could see him as well! She scuttled towards class. But The Weirdy-Beardy Nature TV Presenter followed her! He walked alongside her with a full camera crew! He held a microphone and spoke in a hushed voice.

'Heartbeats beneath the Earth and London's children going grey. Here, we have the icy cold of London City,' he said, tiptoeing along beside her.

'Shoo, shoo!' Amelia said. 'I've got school to go to. You're making it worse.'

The Weirdy-Beardy Nature-Presenter smiled into the camera. 'And this, a Little Girl,' he twiddled his matted beard. 'A Little Girl who has just stumbled into an ancient long-forgotten and beautiful story.'

'Shoo, get away, I don't want true stories,' she flung a glance into the camera-man's camera.

'And I don't want to be a Fruitcake... you're gonna get me in trouble. Go find someone else!' Sergeant Pepper scrabbled to safety in Amelia's musty satchel. Amelia kept her head down and scurried past the boys in the playground. Their eyes looked empty and cold. Their skin was turning grey as lead. They shouted their usual chant at

Amelia that she had a wonky afro. Amelia flushed with shame. 'Leave it out!' she wailed and ran to class before anything more awful could happen. She checked behind her for The Weirdy-Beardy Nature Presenter, but he was gone.

Vanished.

Amelia sunk behind her desk at the back of the class. The bell went and her school teacher sauntered into the classroom. The children's chattering froze in midair.

Mrs Pencil-Sharpener's shoes pointed too far left and right, as though she were about to dive into the pupils and eat them. She preened her facelift higher as she glared at them! Her mouth was pinched and mean.

'It is nearly Christmas, and your first term of big-and-better-school is nearly complete. I hope you have brought your teacher a present?' she said and slid her handbag across the desk aiming to knock one of the children's cans of Diet Joke over with a PING.

Desk lids banged and chairs screeched across the old, scuffed floorboards. Amelia and her classmates groaned watching Mrs PencilSharpener placed several darts in her hair-bun, Amelia winced knowing that they were for throwing at the children later.

'GooooodMooooorning Missssespencilshaaaarpner,' the class chorused. 'Correction!' their teacher barked, her facial expression frozen in a constant glare. 'That's Mrs Pencil-HYPHON-Sharpener!' Amelia groaned and shuffled Sergeant Pepper under the desk with a stale Jammy Biscuit and a bowl of orange squash from her bag. She swore that she would be P for Polite more than ever before in case anyone suspected what might have happened to her today. She tugged at her afro to make it straight and neat. It pinged back into full frizz. She licked her palms and flattened it some more. It pinged back wilder than ever.

'Let things be alright. Just for today!' she prayed. Her bruises were throbbing all over. She lowered herself to sit, but as she did….

Amelia's desk thudded!

And it wasn't Sergeant Pepper.

WA-WOMB.

The desk wobbled on wonky legs.

Amelia held on for dear life, knowing what was happening. But a little voice inside her simply could not believe it. The ground beneath London knew exactly where Amelia was sitting. Of all the seats, in all the classrooms in all the world. Was it an earthquake?

WA-WOMB.

'Oh my goodness' Amelia squeezed her eyes tight shut and crossed her toes in her trainers! If the earth was ALIVE but covered in concrete and cars and STUFF… then maybe the earth… maybe the earth needed to breathe and feel and be free like Amelia Maybe the earth COULDN'T BREATHE.

Amelia grabbed the desk to keep it still. Another gentle earthquake rumbled beneath her desk (almost to agree with her) and threw her school books from her bag and across the floor. Amelia shrieked and scrambled to pick up them up. 'Amelia!' Mrs PencilSharpener screeched.

'But, Miss, my desk...'

'No! Not a word. Nothing weird, nothing strange, nothing loony from you today. No pigeons that have eaten your packed lunch, no grandfather's that have liquidised your homework, please can you all plug your selves into to your computers. You are here to sit still and learn from Miraculous and perfectly pretty Me, your teacher, until you do that, not a peep!' All the children connected their wrists to the computer points on their desks. Data whirred into their brains.

Amelia hit her computer point with a whack and smashed it. No way! She whispered. She looked under her desk. Perhaps there was a rational explanation for the thud. But the desk wasn't attached to anything. No-one was pulling it. She put on her best Everything is Fine face and felt gently under the desk through the soles of her sparkly red trainers. A gentle warm tug seemed to be pulling her body downwards to meet the earth. Amelia leant her chin on her hands and sat very still to maintain her other Not Naughty look, called I Am a Very Good Girl (whilst inside she would usually and secretly grimace or wail and cry). But as usual, to everyone else, she would seem normal... that's with a capital N.

Mrs Pencil-Sharpener tutted and turned to the rest of the class. 'And who has decided what they want to be when they grow up, after last week's disappointing exam results?' she turned to the class scanning the children. 'Edgar Lily? How about you?'

Edgar Lily. Amelia looked over to his desk. All the other kids

said he was weird. She watched him staring at his teacher with large pink unblinking eyes beneath a fine sweep of gloss-white hair. She felt embarrassed for him and stopped looking. She was sure that they only bullied him because of one thing…

'I want to fly to the moon, Miss,' Edgar said, pointing his hand to the sky from his motorised wheelchair.

Mrs Pencil-Sharpener's laughter splurted from her mouth, leaving spittle on her protruding lips.

'Perhaps you would have better luck at the local supermarket checkout, Mr Lily,' Mrs Pencil-Sharpener said. Edgar opened his mouth to speak, but Amelia didn't hear what he said… she was staring at her classmates open-mouthed. Every one of them was ashen grey. The browns, greens and blues of their eyes kept

draining to a neutral grey. They stared up at their teacher, practically hypnotised, Amelia thought. 'I'm scared if I do what they do, I'll lose myself too,' she fidgeted with the holes in her sleeves and cupped her palms to the sides of her face, trying desperately to ignore
London, that seemed to now be speaking to her through the window. She knew what it was saying too. She tried desperately to ignore London. Tears pooled around her eyeballs. I Am an Ordinary Girl and Can't See This, her neck strained to keep her still.

On London's horizon, neon signs advertised the latest plastic Trainers. Adverts flashed on and off for Old Muck Donald's new
crappy Meal's. Industrial chimneys huffed and spluttered. Pointed skyscrapers pierced the clouds and mobile-phone masts shrilled with thousands of voices chattering.
Wa-Womb! Amelia felt the Earth tremble beneath her again...
'What is it that you want from me?' Amelia closed her eyes and whispered inside.
'AMELIA, FEEL THIS,' the Earth whispered back.

Amelia practically fell off her chair.
'The Earth is speaking to me!' she squeezed her face with delight and swung her trainers back and forth. She felt a warmth from the earth light her from within.
'Why are you speaking to me?' Amelia asked.
'You are the one who can feel me.'
Amelia gasped. Not the only one?
She looked around at the hunched shoulders of her classmates fiddling with their whyPhones under their desks and pretending to copy Mrs Pencil-Sharpener's words from the board.

Amelia found herself leaping up, sliding open the lid of her pencil box, and grabbing a handful of stubby felt-tips and snapped wax-crayons. A voice somewhere inside her said, stop it right now or you're gonna get it! but the feeling of love from the Earth was so warm and delicious she just carried on.
Using a fluorescent-green crayon, her eyes big and bright. She leaned toward the grubby window. With a flick of her wrist and a whirr of excitement she traced the shape of the city skyline across the glass. Mrs Pencil-Sharpener continued to whine around the classroom.

Amelia drew around every skyscraper, rooftop and chimneypot. Amelia coloured in the view of London with beaautiful flowers. Yes, I see you. I hear you. I feel you, her heart sang. WA-WHOOM! The Earth's heart beat in return. The grey light coming through the window danced now with her colouring-in colours on the dusty classroom floor. Amelia Firebrand drew enormous green trees sprouting from every road and glorious large flowers from the rooftops. She was so excited that she almost peed. Then, in a wave of excitement, she grabbed her Pocket Book of
Rainbows, and Amelia drew electric bright rainbows springing across East to West London and back again. It was the first time she had not been afraid of the sky falling on her head in years.
'Amelia! Get away from that window; you've ruined the view of the petrol station!' A dart thwacked into the wall half a centimetre away from Amelia's head. Mrs Pencil-Sharpener raced over with a board rubber to wipe Amelia's drawing off of the window.
Amelia dropped her crayons, coming out of her trance.

'What a mess! You're in for it now, young lady. Last week you brought that mangy cat in and now this!' Mrs Pencil-Sharpener grabbed Amelia by her ear.

'But miss!' Amelia's ear burned making her howl.

Mrs Pencil-Sharpener turned on her heel, dropping Amelia who landed back in her chair. Thud! With a swoosh of disgust her teacher returned to write a new heading across the board.

'Class, today we will be looking at my cunning experiment, to prove the cleverness of teachers, with our silly chicken and even sillier rabbit. And YOU, Amelia Firebrand, you can sit in silence plugged into a computer and typing lines for the rest of the day.'

Amelia bit her tongue and slumped in her chair. 'That's what you think,' she whispered under her breath.

Chapter 3

The Stupidity of Rabbits

The children's groan moved like a Mexican wave across the room. Amelia folded her arms and sighed watching the school guinea pig trying to gnaw its way out of its cage.
'As you all know,' Mrs Pencil-Sharpener went on, '...after the baby rabbit was placed with its chicken foster family, the rabbit now searches for food like a chicken, roosts like a chicken and rocks its head like a chicken. It is my aim to prove the cleverness of teachers and The Stupidity of Rabbits.' She wrote it in big letters across the chalkboard.
'Silly bunny!' The class mumbled throwing balls of paper at the hutch. Amelia scowled at her classmates.
'Now let's see what happens when we put the rabbit back in a pen with the foster rabbits. Gather round. Mrs Pencil-Sharpener folded her cardigan over her pointed bosoms.

Amelia peered over from her seat. She saw the three rabbits nestled in the straw. Her heart melted and warmed with a wave of love - and immediately, the ground beneath her shook. Her desk thudded. Amelia held on to her breath. 'Uh-oh here we go again.' She stared at the rabbits. They were the most beautiful creatures she had ever seen. Each had a pair of soft brown eyes that followed her gaze. Amelia's heart beamed… Her desk thudded again. Everything is Fine, Amelia grimaced towards Mrs PencilSharpener's quizzical glare, realising that every time she felt LOVE in her heart - the earth spoke to her. The children's laughing howled in Amelia's ears as they watched the rabbit ignore its old rabbit family and cluck and nest like a chicken, it hopped into a corner of the pen and buried its head under its foot as though it had wings. 'How stupid is that!' the school children cried. 'It doesn't even know what it is. Get it a mirror, Miss.'
Every child in the class was being so mean. Amelia couldn't believe it.
'Miss! It's laying an egg!' The rabbit laid a perfect blue speckled egg in the straw.

The classroom light's reflection quivered in the rabbit's velveteen fur. 'The rabbits scared like me,' she whispered to Sergeant Pepper. And without any more warning, she realised that she could hear the rabbit's heart too. 'Leave me alone,' the rabbit said. She leant closer. Her own pulse walloping hard in her chest.

'Please. Leave me alone. I'm frightened,' the rabbit said.

Mrs Pencil-Sharpener guffawed and pointed at the chalkboard. 'Our experiment has worked. The rabbit no longer recognises itself as a bunny. We shall put it back in its rightful cage, with the CHICKENS. I have proved today, the Stupidity of Rabbits.'

Amelia wriggled in her chair, holding her heart with her palm. She felt the soft swirl of warmth inside her heart from the earth. It made her feel strong. As though she had grown huge tree roots from her feet and connected deep into the ground and as though her crown was touching the sky somewhere up high in the light. But still, the sound of the other children laughing was too much to bear.

'Roast the bunny. Roast the bunny. Eat with chips. Eat with peas. Bunny tails eat with snails. Bunny eyes put in pies. Bunny bum. Fry with plum.'

Amelia's hands trembled, the warmth in her heart drained. She felt cold and scared again; as though there was a frozen ice pop.

T is for Totally Terrified.

Looking around she saw that her classmates' placid grey expressions were changing. Their eyes were darkening, their mouths were scowling.

The bunny backed into its corner, watching the enormous stomping children. Amelia got up and ran behind a large fish tank in the room. She cowered like the rabbit.

'I am like the rabbit.' The realisation hit her like a steam train and whistled in her ears.

'I'm surrounded by chickens and didn't even know that I could be a bunny rabbit.' She stared round at the class, a burning sensation behind her eyes. Her pulse pounded with the pneumatic drill pummelling concrete outside. Amelia gawped, her skin was turning grey too. Not for long though. Amelia squeezed her eyes

tight shut. She breathed light from the sky and above her and a beam of love into her heart, through her shoes, into the ground, beneath the concrete and the pipes - and directly into the Earth.
A surge of light waved up and through her body, right up from her heart to her crown. In that moment EVERYTHING changed. A kaleidoscope of lights bloomed up through the ground beneath London's School for No Good Children, and all at once... AMELIA COULD SEE THE TRUTH IN EVERYTHING.
The rest of the class turned into a bunch of clucking chickens!
Mrs Pencil-Sharpener cock-a doodle-dooed. Amelia fell flatback on her bottom. She rubbed her eyes hard with the soft of her knuckles. Mrs Pencil-Sharpener stood as an enormous strutting cockerel. Plumping and preening with head held high in the air. Amelia looked down at the cockerel's feet... it still wore Mrs Pencil-Sharpener's beige lace-up shoes!
Amelia yelped and hid behind her chair. The children flapped their wings about the room, squawking. She ducked as a giant chicken wearing a school tie flew

over her head and landed on the rabbit pen. At the edge of the classroom Amelia saw Edgar Lily and she realised he was the only one who had not turned into a chicken. The only one! Why? His toothy grin spurred her on.

'Are you listening, child?' Mrs Pencil-Sharpener's crowing voice screeched into the moment.

Amelia stared horrified at her teacher. She shook her head. 'No miss-chicken -sir. I'm not listening to you anymore. I'm thinking. Thinking for myself. Thinking of escape. Thinking of running away,' she yelped in the whirl.

'Well don't.' Mrs PencilSharpener strutted across the room. Amelia ducked behind the classroom fish tank but her teachers black beady chicken eyes stared at her through the brown algae of the sides.

'Look at me, I only got this far in my life by Joining In and Participating!' Her beak tapped the glass. 'Something you're not doing!' A white poop fell out of Mrs Pencil-Sharpener's bottom on to the floor.

An enormous wave of inspiration lit Amelia Firebrand.

She stepped out from behind the fish tank.
'But, I don't want to be like you,' she said to her teacher, the cockerel. 'Or any of you! Whats happening you all are turning GREY!' Amelia's hair sprouted wilder from beneath her bright-yellow-crashhat. Her eyes lit up like a goldfish leaping from its tank and into the ocean for the first time. She felt the eyes of every chicken in the room burning with contempt for her.

Mrs Pencil-Sharpener's perfect knees in perfect tights buckled.

'Outrageous.' She pretended to mop her feathered brow with a Sneezex tissue and swept round from in front of the tank. Amelia was pulled by her arm out across the room.

'You are a bad egg, young lady!' Mrs Pencil-Sharpener cried.

Amelia's heart walloped with pain in her chest.

'Bad egg am I?' she said, her eyes flicking to the blue egg in the nest.

'What would your mother have said?' Mrs Pencil-Sharpener demanded.

Tears twanged in Amelia's eyes.

Her classmates jeered. 'The ugly girl with a wonky afro who lives with her skint Granddad has gone all cross-eyed, miss. She's weird like the rabbit.' The class banged their desk lids and stamped their feet. 'Roast the bunny, roast the bunny...'

Mrs Pencil-Sharpener's voice shrieked through Amelia like a bolt of mains electricity, frazzling her hair.

Amelia squeezed her eyes shut. She clenched her fists till her nails dug into her palms. 'Sergeant Pepper,' she blurted. 'Show them what you've got!' Sergeant Pepper leapt from her desk in a blur of fur and orange.

The class squawked with
laughter. 'Lion! She's got a lion! It's forbidden, it's not allowed!
Roast the lion, roast the lion...' Amelia escaped the classroom.

Sergeant Pepper hissed into a flying fur ball of wildorangegolds, sending all the enormous chickens screeching away from her. Amelia Firebrand tripped, fell and stumbled onwards out of the door screeching down the corridor to the sound of a ringing lunch bell. Catching herself in the cloakroom mirror as she flailed by all arms and legs, she saw that her skin was a rich honey brown warm again. She gasped for breath, wondering how long could she keep from going limp and grey herself?

Chapter 4

Amelia Receives a Message

Amelia skid into the canteen dinner queue. Her pulse was quick. She scanned across the dinner hall. Children sat in chairs wolfing down sandwiches, their grey eyes and discoloured flesh sinking hollow to their bones. A cloud passed overhead turning the entire room fish paste dull. Amelia felt as sad as a pack of bacon. Behind her, a row of young clucking chickens in grey school shoes stood holding dinner trays. They clucked about Amelia. She rubbed her eyes. The insanity of everything was too much. With a furrowed brow, she concentrated on the lunch menu.
Two eyeballs glared up at her from a pork-pie. Amelia looked closer and prodded them with a finger, scrunching up her nose. She looked up to place her order. A gorilla in a dinner lady's pinafore growled at her. 'Chips or peas?'
'Er, chips please,' Amelia blinked. 'A gorilla? What happened to Mrs Bicep?' Amelia looked away. It was as though life was taking

off its sunglasses and she could see straight into its eyes for the first time. Amelia flattened down the tufts of her afro from her crash-hat and tried to stay calm. If she was the only child in London who could feel the Earth – then what on Earth was she supposed to do? She knew she wasn't very clever. Amelia Firebrand NEVER felt clever. But, she was bright enough to know that there wasn't any point in seeing a whole bunch of stuff unless she did something very useful with it. Oh no! What if she got locked up for being weird and seeing the way things were!

A fluttering of comic book pages by the canteen till made her moment of calm come to an immediate halt. She heard voices whispering from the comic books.

'Pow! Bang! Wallop! Wheeee!' Amelia grabbed one and held it to her ear. The voices stopped. She shook the comic again. 'Whhheeeee heee heeee!' it laughed. 'Made you look. Made you stare!' it sang.

Amelia dropped it!

At home-time she cycled back home up Donkey Butter Street, the whizz of the pedals spraying her coat with sludge, the wind stinging her ears. Sergeant Pepper's fur-kissed blanket looked tired and old. Overhead, thick clouds creaked with the weight of the rain like old ships in a storm. Amelia listened to their icy raindrops' squeal with delight, beginning to hurtle to the ground. She shook her head from side to side... It wasn't quite like the time she learnt to ride a bike; but it was a similar sort of feeling. Whatever was happening to her could be either be the most beautiful thing ever or very, very dangerous. She imagined that maybe her brain was uncoiling. Just lolloping out of her ears into a bucket and with it, everything she had ever known.

Her shoulders hunched over her handlebars cradling an ache in her chest. Sergeant Pepper squinted from the bicycle basket bracing his eyes in the wind.

The high-rise tower block, Chewing Gum Gutters even seemed to glared down at her. The sky was turning black. Amelia stared up at the place she had called home all her life. Hundreds of windows lit with flickering television lights stared out over London. Somewhere up high, one resident's very weird garden shed clung like a tick to the outside of the building.

Amelia always worried it might fall on her and squash her flat.

She tightened her crash-hat buckle beneath her cold chin and locked her bike to the railings around the one scraggly tree in the block. Inside, her mind whirred

with everything she had seen, felt and discovered that day. The lift doors closed her into an acidic stench.

'Seventeenth floor,' she heaved to breathe. The lift roared up the shaft stopping only on the thirteenth floor – the floor with the weird shed. The scariest woman in the building hauled herself into the lift, carrying a battered butterfly net. Amelia held her nose with her fingertips. Susan Strange was a bit smelly and burped something eggy.

'Allo Squip! Off to catch some squirrels for dinner,' she rasped. 'There's enough food in this city for an army.'

'Uh-huh,' Amelia shivered and kept her eyes staring straight down at her sparkly red trainers standing in the usual puddle of stale urine in the lift. Amelia eyed the net and the empty pickling jars in Susan Strange's basket, and knew somehow that one day soon she was going to find out what they were for. She'd even heard that Susan Strange was someone's mum! The mum to a little kid that no-one ever saw.

The doors of the lift pinged open and, gripping her nostrils tight, Amelia Firebrand bolted out towards Flat Eleventy-Seven, and sticking her key in the lock, she fell through and into the flat.

Home.

Safe.

For two seconds anyway!

To her astonishment, the door swung to and smacked her behind.

'Gotcha!' it yelled. Amelia yelped and jumped high into the air.

'That is just not ok!' she cried. She stepped into the

hallway, scared about what else she might find.

'Gramps?'

She ignored the welcome mat that moaned about the pee on her trainers.

'Tut-tut!' it said. 'Who's a mucky kid?'

She ignored the egg whisk that beat itself tirelessly on the counter.
She ignored the newspaper which leapt and hid from her down the back of the coat rack. She squealed at Sergeant Pepper. 'Get to my room, please!'
The washing machine in the kitchen drowned her out with loud shrieks. The kettle whistled itself berserk. Amelia jumped up to the living room window. A security camera below winked. She winced and tugged the curtains closed. The glass pane yelled back at her. 'I can't see a thing if you pull them shut.'

Amelia's eyes bulged. EVERYTHING was alive. EVERYHING that she thought was just a big fat nothing... was ALIVE.
Eyeballs in pork pies. Clouds that creaked. Gutters that belched… and an Earth that breathed,
something did soften in her feeling that. Gramps woke up from his armchair. The remote control hopped from his reach back and forth, back

and forth each time he bent round to fumble for it in the chair. It blew raspberries at him with a pink little tongue.

Amelia's insides wriggled with anxiety. He didn't even blink! He couldn't see a thing she was seeing... she WAS mad.

P is for Peculiar.

She stared down at Gramps' newspaper, its headline read, NEW Army Missiles Made Even Bigger Supersize Missiles - Do you want fries with that? the headline guffawed.

M is for Madness.

Amelia's heart beat, she closed her eyes. Something guided her from within. Just like when she'd coloured in the view from the school window. She reached her fingertips to touch the photo of the missiles, she squeezed her eyes tight shut. From the tips of her fingers shone a sparkle of

brilliant lights, the lights danced across the tips of the missiles lighting them with beautiful colours.

M IS for Magic.

Amelia shivered with goosebumps. Hardly daring to look at her hands. Amelia Firebrand

knew, she just KNEW that she had made the missiles useless. Somehow, she had that power. Amelia opened her eyes. Everything was grey and still again. Inspired, she sidled along the wall, backed out of the room, down the hall into her bedroom, and into her bed.
But the bed squealed like a pig!
Amelia scrambled off.
The mattress sighed, 'thank goodness for that, you great lump.'
Amelia pointed back at it with an angry finger.
'I'm not a lump. I'm a... well. I was an ordinary school girl...I'm not sure what I am now.'
Tears sprung from her eyes. She spun round to see her yawning textbooks catapulting themselves out of her bag. Her muddy gym socks leapt into the laundry basket, hissing about going on strike.
She flung the window open for some ice-cold fresh air. Seventeen floors below, car exhausts choked and spluttered. Telephone boxes nattered in shrill voices. Lampposts hopped on the spot to keep warm. All of London had gone completely fruity.

Amelia's insides churned. She pressed her palm to her forehead to check if she had a temperature.

A sparrow opened its beak to sing and the sound of a loud lorry horn honked from it instead. Amelia slammed the window closed.

'ENOUGH!' she shrieked. 'I can't do this. I feel like my head is going to explode!'

Her mobile phone vibrated in her pocket, almost as if it had been listening. She jumped again.

'Look at me everyone, look at me!' it squeaked.

'Shhh, shut-up,' Amelia hopped around the room, battling to keep the phone from wriggling out of her hands. She flipped it open. The phone's blue screen lit her face.

1 New Message from:

The Universe

'What? The UNIVERSE?' Amelia looked down across London at the hundreds of pedestrians, commuters, cars and shops.

She opened the new message and read with wonder…

17th December 3.42pm.
*tHe sTaRs hAvE
bEen wAiTinG foR
yoU tO aWake*

Chapter 5

Amelia Begins to Listen

Airplanes circled the city skyline and a cold north wind yowled
through buildings, down alleys and into Amelia's window.
Amelia threw herself on the bed. Tears howled from her heart like a storm. She knew it.
She'd always known it.
Somewhere deep inside.
She was totally bonkers!
Everything she said so often got a wonky look.
And now this.
The earth and the Universe speaking to her all at once.
What happened to cosy mornings alone in her bedroom, hiding from Gramps with Cow Hoof All the Bits Jelly blancmange for breakfast?
A text message from a prankster at the lie-Phone mobile telephone company?
It must be.
She'd hide. Hide in her room and stare out into the black emptiness of the city sky FOREVER, with aeroplane taillights parading as

stars. Amelia smeared the tears from her cheek and cradled her face, gazing into the big black sky over London.

'I'm bonkers. I knew it – this is proof. Now, no-one will ever be my friend. The night sky above her twinkled light from distant stars and she felt a sigh of relief.

By evening, going in and saying goodnight to Gramps was weirder than ever. She'd tried to tell him.

She had walked into the lounge and there he was, as normal, crumpled in his chair with the telly magazine and a can of B.O. Beer. She couldn't do it, she couldn't be that loony – what if he had a heart attack in response to her stories about children going grey and there being mad gorillas in the school canteen! The anxiety crawled through her skin. What if he might die and Amelia would have No-One-in-All-the-World. For real!

Gramps was asleep in front of the telly, his loud snores echoing around the cramped walls of the flat.

Amelia was feeling exhausted, tired and numb. That night, as the moon rose over London, it was all she could do to zombie out on the torn green sofa and stare into the telly. Her brain in a sort of limbo. Only then did the WeirdyBeardy Nature Presenter walk right into her life AGAIN!

Gramps didn't flinch from his sleep.

But, Amelia's entire body juddered from the sofa.

'Oh arrgh, leave me alone!' she said.

'And this is the home of the lesser-known, Amelia Firebrand,' the television presenter said walking round to crouch down behind a plant in the corner. 'A quiet, shy, creature, unsure of her place in this, the modern wilderness of London city. With just her Gramps for family and a pet cat for a friend, it is little wonder that the small creature is often seen lying awake at night imagining her place in the Universe and where, how and why she fits into it.'

'Go away. I don't want you here. Any of you.' Amelia sighed.

The Weirdy-Beardy Nature Presenter stood up and crossed the room, his fingertips clasped together. 'The rare and LesserSeen-Amelia can often be found foraging for food in the freezer. At night she is kept awake by the howls of police sirens and drunken people in the lift. And, as the truth-of-all-that-is begins to unravel and reveal all around her, her body begins to tremble, to shiver, to shudder, to shake.'

'Go AWAY!' Amelia splurted.

And he did.

Amelia did a quick check. She rubbed her eyes, she rubbed her nose and she squeaked her teeth with her finger to check that she was actually real. Gramps' head fell onto his chest. He gave a small snore. His blanket rose and fell in the dim light. The telly chattered with the evening's headlines. A glamorous lady with pink nail varnish talked about children killed in a warzone. Amelia shuddered and closed her eyes. She listened to Gramps' snores calling and cooing with a low ache.

'Sooo sad,' they sung. 'Sooo sad.'

Amelia opened one eye and stared at him. Was he going to suddenly change again too? The thought of having no grown-up who was safe made her pull her knees up to her chest with a shiver. She held her breath for as long as she could. Gazing at Gramps, she noticed he only had a few twists of grey hair left. His bald head shone in the light of the telly. He looked older every day, she thought. Maybe she would be more than an orphan soon. No family at all. Like in the story books. Was Gramps even family? He barely spoke to her. She pulled at the gold streak in her hair, feeling herself lulled to sleep by the chatter of the television in the corner.

It stood rather forlorn on a battered stand with wheels, its tray stuffed with My Telly Welly magazines. Her chin dropped to her chest. Soon she felt her mind in limbo again, hovering between her everyday life and a deep sleep. Deeep sleeeep. Where everything was ok. Deeeep sleeeeep.

Where no one could hurt her. Where anything bonkers was just a dream.

Stupid text messages. Stupid heartbeats. Stupid madness in her head. She was making it all up. Deeeeep sleeeeep.

Where she could stay safe from the world out there.

Mrs Pencil-Sharpener was right. She'd better start Joining In. It was that or the Looney Bin. Amelia's chin fell to her chest. She was better off forgetting everything.

SLEEEEEP. SLEEEEEP.

Zzzzzzz. Zzzzzzzzzzzzzz.

Deep beautiful silent sleep.

Well that's what she thought!

A high-pitched siren screamed at Amelia to WAKE UP!

Amelia jerked from the sofa.
The television screen was flashing with a dazzling bright light. Amelia shook her head from side to side. The television was speaking. But not from any old telly programme. It hummed with starlight. The words flashed over the telly screen…
WAKE UP. WAKE UP. YOU'RE NOT LISTENING!
'Arrrgh! More?' Amelia grimaced, her teeth clenching tight.
WAKE UP. WAKE UP. The siren got louder.
Amelia clambered to find the remote control.
WAKE UP. WAKE UP.

'I'M AWAKE!' she blurted out.
The alarm stopped. Amelia's ears rang with silence. The room seemed to expand into space

and time. It spoke as if it was an antennae transmission for the UNIVERSE!
Amelia felt very, very small, and very, very alone.

The words on the television screen read:

AMELIA FIREBRAND!
SEE Your FANTASTIC SELF!

And at that:
Amelia Firebrand fell off the sofa.

Chapter 6

The Stars have been Waiting for You to Awake!

The stars shone luminescent bright through the window. Amelia shielded her eyes. 'Stupid moon. Stupid light,' she said and scrabbled for the remote control, stubbed her toe and flumped back face down into the settee.
'What the blooming-heck-a-doodle-custard is going on with that telly!' she said.
'Fantastic Self? It sounds like an 80's pop band! And besides, I already AM my Fantastic Self,' she said, although secretly she absolutely knew that was not true. 'I am really good at loving my cat. I am really, really good at riding my bike. I am even better at gazing out of the window,' as usual her attention drifted.
For a moment everything was calm. Everything was normal. Amelia stood in her normal sparkly red trainers (soiled with chewing gum and trailing a piece of toilet paper), and stared out of the window, dreaming of stars.

A loud COUGH behind her stopped her normalness in a flash. 'A-hem!'
Amelia turned and stared at the telly.
The telly spoke to her in the most un-magic voice she could imagine.
'Oi! I ain't no ORDINARY telly!' it said as though it were some guy at the market selling apples and pears.
Amelia stared. There was something so normal about it the voice that she warmed to it. A creeping and rustling sound from the telly made her stand. She
reached for the lamp but the switch didn't work. She remembered the text message's words again.

The Stars have been waiting for YOU to awake.
The telly screen creaked and crackled. Amelia shivered and pulled her sleeves down over her hands, tiptoeing closer. She caught her breath.
'They don't call me blooming FANTASTIC for nothing!' the telly exclaimed as it bloomed right before her eyes, a golden antique frame appeared with golden leaves and flowers twisting and twined around the reflection. There was something

terrible and beautiful about it at the same time. Like custard, with mustard.

Amelia stared open-mouthed at a swirl of golden bright
handwriting moving across the surface of the screen. A spark of bright light shone through the silhouette of leaves and flowers around it.

See your Fantastic Self

'There's no such thing,' Amelia said, peeking with one eye and shunting closer to it. Amelia was careful to stand to one side so as not to see her reflection. She knew she was ugly with a capital UG. The boys always told her.

Amelia gave the telly a kick (wishing she hadn't) setting it rattling on its old legs. The screen swirled and repeated the words in the golden handwriting...

See your Fantastic Self

Amelia huffed. 'I am not talking to an electrical appliance.' She folded her arms and turned her back on it.

Although, she realised, it was talking to her. And that didn't happen every day. In fact, nothing much had happened ANY day for as long as she could remember.

Until TODAY that was.

'Oh go on!' the Telly said. 'It's worth a shot. What've you got to lose?'

Amelia stuffed a ball of sticky-tape into the television loudspeaker gagging the voice. 'My mind! That's what I have to lose!' But she guessed she had lost that already.

'What if I push that rotten pot plant in front of the screen and see if it can make a reflection of that, instead of a reflection of me?'

Look at your Self...

'Uh tellies don't talk!' She gave it a kick and stubbed her big toe again... really bad. She stuffed some of Gramps' tobacco in her ears so as she couldn't hear the stupid ol' telly. Ha! She grinned. I am the winner.

But the screen shone now sparkling bright, reflecting the moonlight through the window. It's plastic casing transformed into a antique gold frame. Suddenly the screen was a vintage old glass mirror!

Amelia gasped and took down the parched spider plant from the shelf and plonked it down before the mirror, side-stepping away.

'G is for Genius,' she said.

The reflection glinted as though caught in a shaft of sunlight. Amelia rubbed her eyes and looked from the pot plant to its reflection. She clonked herself on the head.
'Oh my giddy Gilbert! It can't be.'
Oh but it can, said a quiet voice somewhere inside her. 'Shhh!' she said out loud. Her eyes boggled. In the telly the reflection of the pot plant had changed. It stood as a thick, juicy green-leafed plant. Flowers dotted it. Honeybees danced on its petals.
'You can't get that at the garden centre...'
Amelia gulped, pink flowers dancing in her ears and tobacco falling out of ears.
'What are you telling me?' she whispered to the mirror, her fingertips warm on its glass. She tried to listen to the magical message. She could almost feel it.
'What is it? That I could be...? A pot plant?' She pulled back.
'Wait... Sergeant Pepper!' Her tom-cat waddled over. He mewed and sat down in front of the magic telly in a soft curl and looked up at his reflection. Amelia watched his one good eye wide with excitement, the other eye stared at the carpet.

With her hands on her hips, Amelia stared. 'How can I resist looking to see what you look like in that thing?' she huffed.
WA-WHOOM!

The earth's heart beat.
Chewing Gum Gutters shook from its foundations. The lightshade above her swung with dust. 'Right! I am going to do this,' she decided. Amelia Firebrand looked around and in at Sergeant Pepper's reflection. She almost fell over when she saw his most Fantastic Self! She always loved his mangy-ness but now she saw him sat proud and strong, not as a fat ginger tom, but as a roaring LION!
'RAAAAAAAH' Sergeant Pepper roared with a mouth of wild teeth.
Amelia's eyes felt as though they had popped out of her head and
somersaulted in the air. 'What the egg-and-spoon?' she said and ungagged the television's speaker fast.
'Sorry Telly,' she said. Magic on a Monday!
'Ooo - here that's better!' the telly said.
'So. Just ONE more thing if I may Amelia...'
'Uh-huh?' Amelia nodded. She looked down at the reflection scribbling fast in even larger

letters, hardly daring to believe what she was seeing.

You're MADE OF MAGIC

Amelia Firebrand

'But I live in Chewing Gum Gutters on a council estate!' Amelia gawped.

You have SEVEN Days to Find Your Fantastic Self...and on the EIGHTH Day Show all the Children of London How to Do the Same.

'WHAT?' Amelia scooped the rest of the tobacco out of her ears.

'In eight days, it's Christmas Day!' She fidgeted in her scratchy school jumper and turned hearing someone clear their throat behind her. The Weirdy-Beardy Television Presenter again. He had popped up behind the yucca in the corner, with a skinny cameraman poking through the leaves.

'And this, poor lonely creature will look at everything in all the world… she will gaze out of any window… dream any dream… anything… but Look into Her Own Eyes'

'Stop judging me!' Amelia said, the corners of her mouth turning down… she sobbed big beautiful tears that shone pure crystaline bright light. She was feeling again.

WA-WOMB!

Amelia sank to her knees, stinging her bruised knees on the carpet and cried for all the world, in all its craziness. She cried for her, for Gramps, for her Mama, for her Papa.

LOOK…

The vintage television whispered.

And Amelia did. She stared puffy-eyed directly into the television's now golden framed vintage mirror.

The ground began to quake. The old black and white photo of Gramps in Jamaica as a young man with his

trousers rolled-up in the sea fell with a clang. Amelia held on for dear life.

WHOOOOOOOSH! A kaleidoscope of colours lit her from within.

The fantastic mirror slid sideways across the room.

'Woooahhhh,' Amelia slid sideways.

In the reflection in the mirror, Amelia saw her Fantastic Self and a LIGHT SO BRIGHT she had to shield her eyes!

The purest clear light illuminated from her! Shooting stars radiated from her heart. She was dancing swirling and whirling wild and free in spinning coloured lights. Amelia's afro whooshed upwards in an invisible rush of pure light energy, her face in AWE.

She saw her own eyes gazing emerald green bright back at her, in shining bright light. And in that moment, she knew that everything was going to be alright. Anything was possible. In all the universe…

Amelia grabbed the plug for the television in the wall and yanked it OUT.

'ENOUGH!' she cried.

The room went black.

And Amelia Firebrand blacked out.

DAY TWO

TUESDAY

18th December

And everything went
quiet...
like a calm
before a storm

Chapter 7

No Child May Enter!

Amelia groaned rubbing her head. What happened? Memories of the night before lingered
and swirled around her. She opened her eyes. Sergeant Pepper sat with his tail curled neatly around his bottom centimetres from her face.
He gazed with a calm steady stare into her eyes. Amelia ruffled the fur on his head and pulled herself up, brushing away a stale crisp stuck to her cheek. Her mind was blank, kinda fuzzy as she looked around.
Gramps chair was empty, a misshapen cushion sat in its usual spot.
A tear rolled down her cheek.
He left me here, she realised, looking down at where she would have passed out on the patterned carpet.
He would have had to step over me!
She turned and pressed her palms

to the telly, it was switched off
and stood cold. She stared in to
its grey glass.
There she was. Plain old Amelia Firebrand.
Grey school jumper. Odd socks.
Red trainers. Same as ever.

Amelia's cry howled out through the sitting
room window and bounced from every building in
London, echoing through every fluorescent lit
subway. Her bones trembled. 'Too much, too
much,' she sobbed. She clutched her Dim Dolly
in one hand and scooped Sergeant Pepper with
the other. He dangled from her arm like a
purring rug. 'I don't want to be something
then nothing. Then nothing then something.'
She covered the telly with the mat from the
hall and sat for hours in Gramps big stinky
armchair staring at the wall.
The clock tick-tocked into the morning. In the
early light, moving shadows of cars and
lorries jigjagged up the walls and across the
ceiling. Morning rose and with it the sound of
wheelie bins being lifted by the council
rubbish lorry. She looked down at her hands
and shoes.

'Hey you, telly,' she gave it a kick.
The telly ignored her. There was no magic writing now. She looked at her brown knobbly knees and her odd socks. She squeezed her eyes tight trying to recollect what she had seen the night before. Her shoulders flumped. Nothing. Then Something.
A sense of lights, of power, of dizzying heights and crashing lows. She stared into the reflection of her eyes, puffy from crying. A fly buzzed round her head. The clock on the mantelpiece grinned at her.
There's More to Come, she felt it say.
Oh no, Amelia thought. Help.
A shriek of police sirens seventeen floors below made Amelia get up to see what was going on. She opened her bedroom window. An ice cold wind whooshed into her face, freezing her ears. Below, the doors to several police cars burst open.
'Wonder who's been bad?' Amelia said turning to face Sergeant Pepper. He placed a soft paw on her ankle. 'Let's get outta here,' she said. 'Maybe we'll check out if Earth is still alive underneath Chewing Gum Gutters.'

Amelia and Sergeant Pepper ran out of the lift and out on to Chewing Gum Gutter's forecourt and hid behind the one tree standing tall and bare in an iron grate. Another London police car roared through the dark street towards the flats.

Its blue siren shrieked. For some reason as the car screeched closer, fear flooded Amelia's belly. She was already scared of the police anyway. They were always so big and tall and she always felt so little and small. Amelia decided to ignore the police chase. There were so many of them around here. They got boring!

She leant down to the iron grating around the old tree.

'Hello tree,' she said and rolled up her sleeve and reached into the patch of Earth that surrounded its trunk. She brushed away crisp packets, cigarette butts and frozen bits of chewing gum from around it. 'No wonder you can't breathe down there,' she said, checking no-one was watching. She patted her fingertips along the gnarled roots of the tree that pushed through the pavement.

'I'm going to try and make things a bit better, she said. 'But I'm really not sure what I can do. I'm just one kid. I've got no friends and I think maybe too I'm a bit ugly.'
Sergeant Pepper squat his orange bottom and weed on the tree.
'Sergeant Pepper!'
She hauled her cat away from the tree.
To her horror, a squeal of lights careered on to the pavement.
She heard a voice belt out from the police car.
'I'm coming to get you! That's right! You've been naughty!'
A speaking car? Amelia stared round blindly into the headlights, shielding her eyes. 'It's talking to me?'
Blue lights raced up and around the kebab shop, newsagent and lampposts. She looked everywhere. No escape! Sergeant Pepper screeched and hid beneath her arms. The lights filled their eyes.
The police car's bonnet roared open into a clanging metallic monster mouth. Amelia stood rigid, rooted to the pavement with fear. She opened her mouth and screamed.

The car screeched on its brakes, and skid across the street. Amelia turned to bolt. Sergeant Pepper leapt away and scrabbled into a skip. In a split second, Amelia checked her north, south, east and west for an escape. Her mind flashed with an image of herself in a straight-jacket rocking in a cell. Her heart thumped against her
ribcage. She felt herself almost disappear from her body with fear. The doors to the police car opened. Four police officers carrying batons stormed towards her.
'What do you want?' Amelia called, running down an alley that turned out to be a dead end. She held on to her ears through her bright-yellow-crash-hat with both hands, twisting her head left and right, up and down. An officer stopped. He reached into his pocket and pulled out a pair of handcuffs.
Amelia blinked. The cuffs ballooned, as big as coiled pythons. Metallic, spiked, with iron chains trawling from them to the ground. Amelia yelled at him that she'd done nothing wrong.
'Oh, contraire,' the officer's eyes gleamed with a wicked twinkle. 'We have it on the

highest authority that you have been accessing a world that you don't belong to.'

Amelia's voice thinned to a squeak. 'What world?' The billions of mad moments since hearing the Earth's heart beating beneath her sparkly red trainers yesterday crashed into her mind along with

the reflection in the telly the night before? Which bit did they mean and how did they even know about any of it!

She took steps back towards a skip.

The officer stepped towards her. His eyeballs twirled with red and white swirls.

Amelia gulped.

The snaking handcuffs opened mouths to reveal hideous jaws.

Amelia closed her eyes. What do I do? she thought as the adrenalin surged through her veins. 'The world in the telly reflection is FORBIDDEN,' the officers shouted.

'It's my telly. I watch it all the time. You can't have it!' Amelia gasped.

'Not any old telly, tho, is it, love? The Prime Minister of

England, Sebastian Peach states in Law 999, that no child may unlawfully enter into divine magical, mystical, mysterious or wondrous experiences.'

Amelia had to be clever. She never felt clever!

'I'll call my Gramps!' she blurted, baring her teeth and growling at them. She glanced up the north face of Chewing Gum Gutters.

'He won't hear you from here.' One of the police officers grinned and snapped his fingers.

The daylight snapped out.

Impossible? Amelia breathed and opened her eyes as wide as she could in the now cold dark. She pressed her palm to her chest, her pulse soaring. It can't be. They can't have the power to do that? Can they?

She heard the officers push each other out of the way to get to her. Amelia's lungs contracted. She took an enormous in-breath and the cavernous space expanded around her.

She plunged into terror. Her mind echoed with the thudding heartbeat she had felt beneath the school paving slabs. Amelia had to trust in something GOOD! She breathed deep and imagined a bright light shining over her from

the universe and down her legs to her feet.
Down to the ground. There it was.
Wa-Whoom!
Under her feet. The same thud. The Earth was speaking to her.
A surge of crystalline light whooshed up and into Amelia. The Earth was alive and speaking... through her!
Amelia found words streaming from her lips. Words she didn't understand. A beautiful prayer. From a place beyond her here. Her spine tingled. She leapt up high. Beautiful words! Words that brought the daylight back.
"*****************" she sang, trilling like a bird. The street lit from beneath the cloudy sky again.
The ground shook. The scrambling officers wobbled. One tripped. One slipped. Amelia's arms spread like a scarecrow to stay upright. The words singing from her lips could only be saying one thing, she felt it.
LOVE IS ALL THERE IS!
The brick walls around her shook.
Amelia turned to look at falling debris. Lampposts wobbled. Pigeons scattered. With a huge rumble of ground and buildings, the tired

bare old tree outside Chewing Gum Gutters started to shake.

Amelia gasped.

The police officers squealed.

The tree leant over and down, leaning a branch of fingers out to Amelia.

'B-boom,' she felt its heartbeat too.

Amelia ran into its enormous twig fingers.

Sergeant Pepper poked his whiskers out from the skip.

'You can't do that!' Amelia heard the officers wail. 'It's impossible! The Impossible is forbidden under Law 999 sub-section B…'

Amelia stared down as she was lifted by the tree high up beside Chewing Gum Gutters. She rushed with excitement.

'We have to get back to that telly!' she yelled.

It's more than a VIP... it's a
VIT! That's a Very Important
Telly!'

Sergeant Pepper had leapt on behind her. He dangled from her jeans with crazed claws, his bright orange tail curling and reaching wild as a monkey for safety.

'Tree! Can you put me back in the window with the Fantastic Telly in it?' Amelia shouted.

A low loud rumble from the heart of the tree nodded in agreement.

Amelia found herself yelling words again, they were flowing through her from all of the stars, the earth the rivers the waterfalls the ocean, the sea.

"*****************'' she sang, chirruping loud as a thousand birds and waving to the officers, tiny as ants beneath her.

Chapter 8

Trapped in a Shed of Pickled Parts

With a huge thwack!!! Amelia and Sergeant Pepper were hurled by the tree through a small window. Amelia screamed, her jeans tearing and her thigh catching on a nail. Sergeant Pepper yowled.

'Yeooow! Dark, dark, dark. Don't like the dark.'

It was dark and dank.

They tumbled to the floor. A stomach-curdling creak made Amelia realise that she was standing on weak, wobbly floorboards. Goosebumps broke out on her forearms. A pungent odour of old socks and vinegar filled her nostrils. Sergeant Pepper growled. He plopped down with soft paws.

'They turned the daylight out...how? And, the old Chewing Gum Gutters tree… it helped us!' Amelia said to him in the shadows. She checked her thigh, a thin cut wept blood, but she was OK. She dabbed it with some dribble on a finger.

'That magic love light came from the Universe and love came through me! Although', she said suddenly looking around: 'who knows where we are now.'

Sergeant Pepper let out a small but significant fart.

Amelia felt with her palm over the wooden walls, splinters of rotten wood caught at her soft fingertips. Only the window they had fallen through gave them any daylight. Her forehead was sweating. She didn't feel safe. She never felt safe!

The floorboards they stood on were quaking. Wherever and whatever they were in, it wasn't stable.

A crack in the wooden door flickered with a blue light. Amelia hopped over Sergeant Pepper and pressed her face to the frame. She could see someone's front room on the other side of the door, lit by a floral lamp. The room looked cluttered by years of bric-a-brac and hard upright armchairs.

'Worse than Gramps' stuff,' she thought scowling at china horses. 'Where are we?'

A small dog yapped from another room. Amelia cast her eyes over brass ornaments. Coasters

from seaside towns. Dolls in ornamental jars. Two square windows, draped in floral brown curtains told Amelia
roughly where she was. Somewhere back inside Chewing Gum Gutters. The windows were unmistakable, identical to hers and Gramps. She was in a neighbour's flat.
But whose?
Amelia's palms splayed like starfish. Through the crack she could see a bulging woman sitting in a pink pinafore with pink rubber gloves. Amelia shuddered. It was that beast of a woman who she saw in the lift, who usually walked the corridors, her eyes boggling, with a spray can of Spider Spit polishing the window ledges… Susan Strange.
Susan sat cutting her toenails into a butter dish. The nail clipper pinged a big toe nail from it at a hundred miles an hour and right through the lock into
Amelia's spying eye.
'Yow!' Amelia said under her breath. She looked again to see Susan cross the room to pet her wicked-eyed Pekinese. The Pekinese stood up and followed her over to a hallway

just out of Amelia's view. Amelia peered to see better.

Susan Strange stood in the hall doorway dragging something into the
room. Her limp greasy hair straggled down over her eyes.

Amelia huddled down by the crack in the door and stared through at Susan Strange who was flexing her bulbous biceps. Sergeant Pepper crouched ready to pounce from Amelia's feet.

Susan Strange began dragging a television into the sitting room.

Amelia squashed her face hard against the crack to see better. A battered television on a stand with wheels stuffed with My Telly Welly magazines!

The Fantastic Television!

'What the heck? She's nicked my telly!' Amelia's stomach churned. She watched as her television was wheeled into the middle of the room. Susan stopped to rub her hands with glee then reached into her pink pinafore pouch. She pulled out a large meat hatchet. Light glinted along the blade. Susan Strange heaved it up, her face contorted with the effort.

Amelia shrieked. 'The Fantastic Telly! No! I want to see my Fantastic Self!' She jumped back a step and clamped her hands to her mouth.

On hearing the din, Susan Strange took four thumping steps towards the door and from out in the sitting room flicked a switch.

A bright light bulb hanging from a dusty wire lit above Amelia's head.

Amelia winced in the super white bright. She squinted to see where she was. She was in a rickety old shed. The shed clinging to the side of Chewing Gum Gutters! And the tree that put her and Sergeant Pepper here knew that she needed to be here to see the telly about to be destroyed.

Clever tree!

Looking round she saw that stacked inside the shed on rows of shelves were hundreds of glass jars. The Butterfly net she saw Susan carrying in the lift! Each jar was misted with purple, pink and blue liquids. Each one bore a label.

Aghast, Amelia mouthed the words…

The Shed of Pickled Parts!

Londoners' Stressed Smiles

Londoners' Fumey Nostrils

Londoners' Pickled Pets

Londoners' Burst Bunions

Londoners' Irritable eyes

Londoners' Brittle Bones

Londoners' Melted Muscles

'She's as mad as green custard!' Amelia said. 'She has her own homepickling-set-up and eats those pickled bits of Londoners for her dinner!' she shivered, feeling goose bumps fleck her arms.

Susan's hatchet hand twitched. Then, a large thump on the shed door made Amelia and Sergeant Pepper freeze like ice pops. A gruff and harrowing singing voice sounded through the door from Susan Strange.

'London is almost dead, there's nothing left alive. If only there was some love in your life. Some of you might survive.'

Amelia shuddered. Her bones pattered with the memory of the Earth's beating heart under London. Where was the magic now? Amelia was now seeing movement in the jars. Things were still alive in there! Revolting putrid sluggy matter. The remnants of trawling through dustbin gravy… or worse. Amelia wondered.

A small porthole window in the shed door flipped open. Susan Strange's gammy face glared inside.

'BURGLIERS!' Susan Strange roared. 'There's a burglier in my shed! A child burglier no less!' Susan stomped from one foot to the other in a strange dance.

'That's right,' she bellowed.

'You'll be locked in for the night… Find me a child that's not as lazy as tripe. That does its homework every night. That washes between its fingers and toes… But there's no such child, as everyone knows!

They're liars and fibbers.

They're rotten to the core. They're dead inside. They're gonna get what for! But the Pickled Parts – they get top score. I can see you're a problem. I can see you're not right. I'm going to lock you in the shed…London will lose this fight!'

Amelia ducked down low feeling the shed shudder as Susan slammed another bolt across the door. 'Nothing in there except bits and pieces of revoltingness!' Susan said and dropped the hatchet.

Time yawned into an eternity for Amelia. She shuffled and fidgeted, scratched and pondered and slowly her eyes adjusted to her surroundings. She clutched at her chest. Memories of her Mama coming to the surface of her mind. Questions about her Papa and his giving her up as a little baby.

Amelia felt glum as gluepots. The grizzly grey of the clouds and the honeycomb orange of London's streetlights at dusk filtered through cracks in the wood. She could now vaguely make out rows of pickling jars. An eyeball floated like a pickled onion and glared at her.

'Let me OUT!' in a squeaky shout, she pounded the shed's floorboards with her small fists, wondering how many floors high she was from a grim and horrid death.

Three jars on the shelves slipped and smashed to the floor. Gruesome slithery slatheries slimed across Amelia's feet. Splinters of wood split beneath her and twanged their way down seventeen floors to the pavement below.

Susan Strange plugged in Amelia's Fantastic television. Amelia watched fascinated. Would Susan Strange have a Fantastic Self too?

Amelia watched the shadows creep across the shelves. She peered at
the Pickled Parts floating in jars all around her. The gloopy formaldehyde hung with Londoners' ails along with lifeless squirrels furs, frogs' limbs and pigeon's eyes. Suspended in the fluids they held an eerie calm.

'What does she mean, London will lose the fight?' Amelia shivered.

'I'm trapped. A captive! Dead meat. I can't do anything for London now.' She slumped into a corner, pulling her knees in tight and tugging her school jumper over them to keep herself warm. Sergeant Pepper clambered up and around her, curling around her neck, like a giant warm purring scarf.

Amelia Firebrand felt some relief.

'Thanks, 'Sarge.' She closed her eyes and went to sleep.

Day 3

Wednesday

19th December

Chapter 9

The Beautiful Uglies

Amelia woke up. Her stomach growled. Her body ached. She was colder than she had ever been. Her teeth chattered and her eyelids dropped heavy as lead. She slumped against the shelving.
Dark words froze in her mind. Frightened. Scared. Alone. Dying.
'I need the light to come again, the LOVE of the Universe, my Fantastic Self... anything.'
But Amelia felt AWFUL! Amelia's mind spun with fear stories and terrible endings thoughts of catastrophe raced in her mind. Would Gramps be worried about her? She should be heading off for school by now with Sergeant Pepper wrapped cosy on his skateboard. Would the police still be looking for her?
What was that smell? Eugh, formaldehyde. The stuff grown-ups pickled raw animals with in museums. Jars had fallen in the night. They

lay broken around her. Pickled newts splayed in dramatic positions. Spread-eagled squirrels baked and pinned. Splattered hedgehog combed and ironed. Stuffed worms, lumpy as gherkins. Amelia knelt down, sweeping aside broken glass with an old newspaper to look at them all. She squeezed her eyes closed, feeling the grief that each of them had had a heartbeat too. The bearded nature presenter scrambled up from a tired old box in the opposite corner. Amelia scrabbled further back with surprise. 'Stop following me!' He wore a hunter's cap today and shed coloured camouflage. He tapped his microphone.

'And this tiny girl creature, cold, lifeless and sad still hasn't fully understood what is happening to her. She must come to understand it, as without her, London will not survive.'

'What???,' Amelia said.

'She would have the key to the most powerful love of the entire universe,' he whispered with a finger to his lips. 'If she knew that SHE was the one that could allow it all into being.'

Amelia turned her back on him. 'What are you talking about, imagining the Universe into being?

I'm ten-and-three- quarters, don't you know.' She stared up at the roof. Her heart sank into her stomach. She tugged out her purse and unzipped it, pulling out the only photo she had of her Mama. It was curled at the edges. Her Mama's smile was starting to fade.

'Stupid ugly me, in stupid ugly London, in a stupid ugly shed with a stupid ugly lady outside the door.'

The photo had always been torn in half.

In the photo, along the tear, a thin sliver of a man's brown trouser leg nestled next to her Mama on a park bench in her beautiful blue dress.

'Papa?' She'd never even seen his face.

Tears erupted from her eyes.

She had never known him. She had never known who he even was.

'I hate that I can't control any of this!' she wailed into her lap.

Sergeant Pepper jumped up and wrapped himself around her neck. 'And I hate you too, Sergeant

Pepper. Yes, I hate you!' she scrambled up and pulled him off of
her. He leapt to the floor with a yowling meow and hid in a corner.
'Get me out!' she screamed. 'Get me out! I hate this. All of it.' Her cheeks burned and her eyes were red raw. Her hands scrabbled to tear off her bright-yellow-crashhat. 'And get this off of me. Nothing plastic will keep me safe!'
Spit flew from her mouth and snot flew from her nose. Her lungs heaved. Just before she had time to take it off, it happened...
Wa-Womb.
The Earth's heartbeat.
There it was.
There it was again. A slow, rhythmic thud.
A heartbeat.
The walls trembled.
Amelia stopped. She looked up from her sodden sleeve.
Something was happening.
Something inside her. She felt the familiar warmth of light rising up and through her heart from the Earth. Filling her up with a whoosh of love.

'Love? The Universe feels like Love.'
Around her, she felt a glimmer of awareness, as though the Pickled Parts were watching. She stared at them. Her heart was opening. Her sight was getting clearer. As she felt different... they started to change.
She rubbed her eyes. They didn't look so ugly after all, just a bit sad and droopy. Sergeant Pepper came back out from the corner.
In the jars of Pickled Parts, eyeballs twizzled in their gloop to stare round to her. Amelia flinched, her back pressing harder into the wall. Limbs shunted against one another to reach for her. The shelves rattled. The lid of a jar unscrewed with an eerie squeak. A slime covered, tentacled beasty crawled from it, three antennae reached towards her with despair.
A blue tongue waggled itself free.
Amelia jolted upright.
The hideous parts in the jars were all writhing towards her. They swelled with the glory of being alive again.
Amelia shuddered, hopping back and forth to avoid them, her heart deflating with horror. Things were touching her skin. She pulled the

tear of her jeans tight so as they couldn't touch her cut.

Horrid oozy things were alive and wanted to eat her! She backed towards the shed door. Gruesome grizzlies mulched along the floor. Putrid slugs of matter yawned with mouths full of teeth and rot. Amelia wriggled as far as she could against the door.

'Have I made you come alive?' she asked. Yes, came the reply from the love inside of her. Yes.

The bearded nature presenter pulled out an old-style filming camera and pointed it at Amelia in the action.

'Will she discover that her own body, heart and soul hold the blueprint to it all... the secret to life itself?

Will she let her fear feed the Uglies that want to hurt her?'

'Ohhh SHUTTUP! Yeeeeas. Eugh. Ouch. Eeeek.' Leeches sunk their pointed teeth into Amelia's ankles. Amelia jumped. 'Owwwwww. Not fair. Not fair.'

She grappled with a moving jar on the shelf and yanked it from its sluggy comrade. She hurled the jar at the writhing mass on the

floor. Amelia jumped to the left. She pressed her palms to her ears. What
if Susan Strange heard? Amelia would be dead as a dodo!
'What are you?' she wondered and squinted to read some more of their labels. Along with Londoners' miserable bits, they were London's wildlife too. Squirrels. Rats. Pigeons.
Amelia sat down in the sludge of the shed. She concentrated on calming herself. But her mind leapt from one thought to another, like a deranged monkey. She let each thought drift up into the rafters of the shed. A peace settled in her mind. With her mind quiet she could sink deeper into her tired body. With her mind quiet she could sink into the bruises and bumps, the ocean of tears and feel a deeper peace.
With her mind quiet... her HEART exploded OPEN.
Wa-Whoom!
Wa-Whoom!
Wa-Whoom!
The heat in her surged, a volcanic magma of LOVE rocketed inside her, and...
POW!!!

In the shed... each of the creatures was transformed.

Amelia's eyes ballooned huge as globes watching.

Bobbing ugly limbs became winged and graceful. The rolling eyeballs flit up from the ground to wink. Spinning mid-air with a full spectrum of coloured lights they too grew delicate wings. Amelia bathed in the light of the curious creatures, all humming, all singing, and all bright.

'All things bright and beautiful...' she sang, grinning with a new version of the old school hymn.

Feathered wings appeared from all the Uglies. Red raw snotty noses, thumping sad hearts suddenly filled with life again. Crawling limbs, dried pigs' ears, long toes, bunny brains sprouted before her. They sparkled with light. Amelia danced beneath them, reaching her hands out to touch them.

'You are all so lovely and ugly,' she said thinking of how she normally even hated her own reflection. 'With this Love, I can change everything and anything.

I've got this Fantastic Telly. It's out there now, I wonder if I can learn how to see this Love myself?' she nodded to the other side of the shed door. 'It's been showing me how what I thought was ugly is actually full of magic and beauty and stuff.'
'Maybe you'll help me?'
The swarm of Uglies hummed in agreement.
'Thank you.' Amelia smiled, holding out her palm for a two legged nose to perch on. The nose took a deep breath as if to sing, but instead sneezed. 'How do we get out of here?' Amelia looked through the lock. Susan Strange waddled into the living room with a pair of Fluffy Bunny pyjamas on and bobtail slippers. A loud ring from the telephone made Susan spill her cup of tea.
Amelia winced watching the tea splash on to her Fantastic television.
Susan Strange picked up the phone. 'Strange Household,' she said. 'Chewing Gum Gutters.'
'Strange indeed,' Amelia said.
She watched Susan suddenly straighten, standing stiff as a board. 'Yes your Prime Ministerlyness, Sebastian

Peachlyness, your most Highliness, I have it here.' Susan's one good eye boggled at the telly. 'I'll destroy it at once.'

Amelia tried to see what she would do next. Who was she talking to on the telephone? The Prime Minister? Surely that was impossible?

Susan walked over to the settee and grabbed her hatchet.

Amelia's skin iced with goosebumps. 'Oh my gawd.'

Susan lifted the hatchet high above her head, ready to smash the Fantastic television into smithereens. Amelia held her breath. Had the tree brought her here to see this? To see the Fantastic television destroyed? Was this what the police had wanted?

Susan bellowed, 'No more sickywicky goody-woody niceness in London.' She raised the hatchet high and plunged it downwards.

Amelia's insides screamed. She clamped her hands over her mouth so as not to make a sound.

Susan Strange stopped. The hatchet hovered millimetres away from the telly. Something had stopped her. She wobbled on the spot as though an arrow had shot her and lowered the hatchet, stooping down to look at the television screen.

The screen hissed white noise.

Amelia watched Susan look over her shoulder and then back at the screen.

Susan gave the telly a prod with a bunioned finger.

'Hellooooo.' she said. 'Anyone in there?'

Amelia gawped with utter fascination. Susan Strange hadn't smashed the telly. She was talking to it!

The front door banged open behind Susan Strange who jumped knee high into the air and landed with a crash.

'What the blinkin'..?' said Susan Strange.

'Oh… it's you,' her face dropped seeing who it was. 'Mum, what's for breakfast?' Amelia heard a boy's voice say.

Susan growled, 'Bland Flakes,' and lifted her hatchet above the telly.

Amelia stared. The small boy was Edgar Lily! Her body raced with adrenalin. She stumbled in the shed, grappling for one of the Uglies' tails. 'That's Edgar Lily's mum?'

'What's that noise?' Edgar Lily asked as Amelia heard the wheels of his chair spin across the room.

'Burgliers!' Susan Strange cried. 'Leave them in there to rot like old cabbage in the gutter.'

Amelia looked up at the porthole window. Edgar Lily's huge pink eyes gawked in at her. Kind, curious and sad. He spun back from the window. Amelia heard him shouting.

'You can't keep, Amelia Firebrand in there, mum!'

Amelia's eyes sprung with burning tears as a commotion of arguing ensued. Amelia tried to block her ears, but couldn't, her stomach reeled.

Edgar Lily was whalloped across the room. He bounced back, shaking himself too. 'Mum what the heck are you doing? Put that axe down.'

Susan stood on a wobbling tea trolley, the hatchet high above her head, ready to strike. Amelia squeezed her eyes closed. Her eyelashes reaching soft to her cheeks.

Wa-Womb.

She consulted the love and light in her heart. Listening deep. Cutting through the noise outside the shed, she found comfort in the calm voice within her.

The voice was silvery soft and flooded her whole body with peace. In her imagination gentle words and colourful images danced. They whirled and merged and, as if by magic, created a plan. She opened her eyes wide and reached into the corner of the shed for a spool of thread and whispered to the Uglies of her Big Plan.

One by one the Uglies allowed her to loop a double-bowed thread around their middles. They dangled from them soft and strong as spider webs from lampposts in the morning mist.

Amelia tapped a flying pickled newt on its tail to start the plan. It understood at once and flew to the shed door bobbing up and down with its new thread. The newt slipped through the door lock and used its shrivelled tail to undo the lock.

The door opened with a gentle squeak. Amelia winced and peered out at Susan, who now stood on the settee; her chunky ankles sunk low into the upholstery.

Amelia felt the Uglies buzz with anticipation. She gave the nod. One by one the Uglies swarmed up and
over and out through the door, heebie-jeeebieing into the room. Amelia leapt out behind them cawing and squawking. She didn't have time to worry about the enormous hatchet and the damage it could cause her.
In front of her Edgar Lily spun around out of her way.
Susan Strange's mouth contorted into a wide O. She yowled with horror. The Uglies flew towards her in a frenzied mass. Amelia grabbed a lampshade to protect herself, but looked on amazed. She had not known or been told from the whispers in her heart what would happen when the Uglies met Susan.
To her delight the Uglies quivered across her skin, rippling, tickling her arms, her head, her tummy. Susan shrank back in horror and she scrunched up into a giant bulbous ball on the carpet and shrieked for them to leave her alone. Amelia stole her chance the Fantastic Telly was within diving distance. She leapt for it, landing with a clang.

Susan's arm lurched forwards. Amelia skirted it. She whistled loud to the Uglies.

'OK. Now!' The Uglies whizzed to the telly, whirling threads around
it, hoisting it into the air. Susan's hatchet swung for Amelia's head. She ducked. It thwanged into a wall beside her. From nowhere Edgar Lily appeared hauling her on to his chair and whizzing her towards the front door.

'Hello!'

Amelia grinned and leaning forward tugged the front door open. The Uglies levied the telly down the hall. Edgar Lily tore down the hallway, helping Amelia to escape. The wheels beneath them spun like Catherine wheels. They raced through resident's bin liners, Ploppers Baked Bean cans tearing the black plastic and rolling down the hall.

Through an open window in the hallway, the Uglies swarmed up and over London. Susan Strange roared down the hallway after Amelia and Edgar, who had just seconds to leap out after them.

'Go, Go!' Edgar cried.

Amelia leapt on to the window ledge and looked down. The pavement below loomed with sudden plunging death. Her hands and legs spread eagled, she turned to wave at Edgar Lily and leapt forwards out into the night. She grabbed the Uglies' strings, clutching and grasping at them with terror in her eyes.

She shimmied herself up the Uglies' threads. Her body's weight caused a sudden drop in Uglies' flight, but she held tight and clung with little gripped fists. She turned to see Susan Strange beating the air from the window, her monobrow wriggling with rage.

Amelia dangled as though being swept away by a clutch of deranged balloons. Her body stretched downwards like cookie dough. The Uglies whooped and farted, sneezed and sprayed her with snot and wafting great stinks over London.

Amelia's palms stung from their tugging threads, her legs dangled. She waggled her legs to hoist herself up closer towards them. Down below, cars and lorries crawled along in snail trails of exhaust-fuming traffic. The occasional pedestrian glanced up at her not knowing what she was. Turning and looking away.

'Over there, that way!' Amelia yelled up into the freezing cold morning sky. Her fingers and toes numbed.

The possibility of leaving London was so enticing, she could leave.

Just fly away! The thought of her Gramps, no matter how horrid he had been panged in her throat. She knew that they had to get the Fantastic Telly back to the flat and tell Gramps everything. If he'd even noticed that she had gone. The Fantastic Telly would be able to show Gramps his Fantastic Self too. The Uglies hummed in agreement as though reading her thoughts. They curved round and headed back to Chewing Gum Gutters. A hundred television aerials silhouetted by clusters of lit windows and washing lines was their only guide. Chewing Gum Gutters' rooftop, littered with rusted shopping trolleys and a large fire exit, loomed beneath Amelia's dangling shoes.

'Lower!' she yelled, and let go, crashing into a tarpaulin. Her legs buckled beneath her. Amelia firebrand somersaulted into a pile of old chip fat tins left on the roof, their gunk exploding over her.

The Uglies swarmed down behind her with the telly. It touched the ground with a soft donk. Amelia jumped up, paling the oil off of her and helped, catching a glimpse
of a morning moon in the Fantastic Telly's reflection.
She untwined the Uglies' threads, until they were all safe and ready for the next step. She crossed her fingers and toes that Gramps would either love all this or he would be snoring away in his chair and they could sneak the telly past him into her room... for now.
They whirled down the fire escape stairwell. Amelia marvelled at the weirdness of the hovering telly carried by the Uglies shimmering and sparkling in the dim light of the hallway. A grease smeared window of Flat Eleventy-Seven let in a slant of turgid light on to the dusty floor. Amelia squished her nose to the glass. Outside, Susan Strange scurried across the forecourt looking this way and that for the cloud of Uglies, Amelia and the telly.
Amelia shivered. 'You can't catch me,' she whispered placing both her hands protectively over her heart.

Wa-Womb.

Wa-Womb.

Wa-Womb.

Amelia listened for Gramps and pushed open Flat Eleventy- Seven's
front door. At once, Gramps' bald head peered round from his arm chair. When he saw the cloud of Uglies swarm into the room ahead of Amelia he leapt up and hobbled for the kitchen cupboard under the sink scuffing along in his old tartan slippers.

'The Bug Erase! Quick! Swarm! Murder! Mayhem! We're all gonna die.'

Amelia was amazed he hadn't even stopped to see if she was all right. He had just run off! She stood clutching the telly, waiting for the Uglies to settle. She watched. A fat nostril perched on the back of Gramps' armchair inhaled deeply and sneezed with a snot-filled roar.

An eyeball twizzled along the carpet just out of reach of Sergeant Pepper who swiped at it with a claw. Gramps hobbled back into the room with the Bug Ease, set to spray them all.

'Where've you been with my telly?' he said and unleashed the full force of the Bug Ease.

The moment a spray of the Bug Ease's toxic mist hissed from the aerosol, the Uglies lashed into the
air, gnawing, hissing, and biting the air.
'Arrgh! They're the most disgusting things I have ever seen!' Gramps yowled, his face crinkling like a crisp packet.
The Uglies hummed back in unison. 'You're pretty revolting yourself, old man.'
'You can speak?' Amelia blurted to them.
Gramps spluttered, leaping into the air. 'You rotten maggots. You pathetic ugly squits… Why I'm gonna squash you all and dump you all in the gutter where you belong.'
Amelia had had enough. She stomped her foot on the carpet.
'STOP!' she said. 'Gramps. Get used to it, 'cos this lot of beauties just saved my butt from a fate worse than death…and we got the telly now so we are back in the game.'
'What game?'
Amelia wheeled the telly up to him. 'Gramps we've got ourselves one, Fantastic television,' she beamed.

Gramps rubbed the bristles on his chin, pulling his old cardigan closer. 'What do you mean… a fantastic telly?'

Chapter 10

Gramps' Terrible Secret

'Hang on, 'Melia, I'll get me glasses!' Gramps said with an unusual burst of enthusiasm. Amelia watched Gramps hobble from the sitting room. The back of his trousers sagged into a sad smile. She took a big deep breath. It was the first time she had ever felt his interest in anything she had ever said. The first time. Her shoulders sank and she pulled her jumper tight.
The Fantastic Telly looked as normal as any old bit of junk you could get in a skip. She rested her hands on its surface. 'Hello,' she said. 'Hello. Are you going to show me again my Not ugly Me? I'm kinda getting it, that when I feel horrid, I feel ugly and then when I feel happy I feel not ugly, and full of JOY.'
The Uglies settled about her as autumn leaves nestle a storm-swept tree. Their breathing had

calmed from their flight. They now sat in a gentle whisper of wings. She could just make out the slow patter
of their limbs along the floor. Sergeant Pepper jumped into Amelia's arms. The warmth of his heavy body soothed her for a moment. She looked out the window over to her school. It looked as small as a bowl of soggy Bland Flakes.

Downstairs Edgar Lily steamed across the open courtyard in his motorised wheelchair. His scarf flapped in the wind behind him on his way to school. A flock of grubby pigeons took off in a flurry of feathers in fright.

Maybe Amelia and Edgar were as odd as each other.

'N is for Normal,' she whispered. 'But maybe normal isn't all that it's cracked up to be. Maybe everyone is U for Unique.' She remembered the telly's words crystal clear. 'See your Fantastic Self.'

Sergeant Pepper looked up at her quizzically. 'I know, I know.' She slumped her head into her hands. 'I'm too scared. Who was that girl in the Fantastic Telly?'

Sergeant Pepper nudged her arm with his nose.

'I don't want to. Don't make me,' Amelia pleaded and placed him on the carpet. She raised her hands to her face.

'Don't make me look at it.' Tears rolled down her cheeks landing in Sergeant Pepper's fur. 'I'll look at my Fantastic reflection again when I'm ready.'

Although it did occur to her that perhaps the telly might have been Fantastic only just that once. What if she had been through all this...to discover that it was as ordinary as all the other tellies in the building? Hmmm. She stared at it.

Hmmm. She stared at it some more and plugged its socket into the wall. Hmmm. It wasn't the first time she had gotten something wrong - she sat back up and hit her head - realising that it wasn't going to be the last.

She switched on the telly.

A surge of power and the telly hummed into life. The screen lit up with a grey fuzz. Amelia ducked. And listened.

'And this morning, on Big Ben News all the latest of London's miserable and despairing stories!'

Amelia sighed with relief.

'Ahhh Normality.' She felt herself relax, a wave of relief washing through her tired muscles.

She wasn't sure if this meant she was safe now or whether she should be sad that the telly was just as it had always been.

Nothing Fantastic about it?

She stared into the screen at the newsreader, Roy Rupert Randolph Rogers and his wonky hairpiece, and fumbled for the remote to change the channel.

In the time it took her to flick her eyes down and look back up, everything changed.

Wa-Whoom! Her chair rumbled. Wa-Womb!

The screen flashed bright and lit Amelia's face with its glow. She shuffled back and felt tears of love spring to her eyes. She couldn't bear to go back to how life had been before really.

Gramps shouted from the kitchen. 'Think someone's hidden me glasses!'

Amelia turned quickly, wrenching her neck. The Uglies took flight into the corners of the ceiling.

Gramps called again.

'Ammmeeelia!'

Before Amelia had time to think of how she would explain everything to Gramps that quick... the door handle turned. She twisted. The door hit the wall with a bang. Gramps stared into the Fantastic Telly.

Oh crikey!' Amelia gasped and leapt to the torn green sofa. She hadn't explained any of his yet! She tugged Gramps' raggedy patchwork blanket off and hurled it towards the screen. It missed and crumpled to the floor.

WA-WOMB! The whole flat shuddered.

Gramps' withered face filled with terror staring into the screen. 'Who's that in that telly?' he blurted.

'I...I don't know Gramps, I can't see,' she said.

His knuckles were white around his walking stick.

'Who the heck is that?' he demanded.

In his reflection Amelia saw a proud man.

'It's you, Gramps!' she cried.

The Gramps in the reflection beamed out at him with a huge radiance of light from his chest and a broad welcoming smile. He
stood strong, full of life.

'That's not me, Amelia,' Gramps' face strained. 'You're a magnificent man, Gramps!' Amelia surged with joy. But when she turned to look at him - he was staring up at the ceiling - at the swarm of Uglies.

The Uglies took flight and filled Amelia's bedroom in a blurred frenzy.

Gramps squeaked, dropped his stick and ran out into the corridor.

'Gramps, Gramps? Come back,' Amelia yelled, through cupped hands.

The hall echoed with his deep wail. Amelia's whole being shuddered. He sounded like a wounded fox out at the bins, lost in the night.

Amelia followed Gramps into the sitting room. He slumped into his chair, pulling off his floral tapestry slippers and letting his curled toes relax on the carpet. His breathing was way too heavy for his rickety lungs, Amelia thought. She watched his hands tremble in his lap.

'I've got something to tell you, Amelia,' he said.

Amelia blinked.

Gramps took a deep breath. 'That reflection means more than you can know,' he said. He reached under his chair and pulled out a tattered brown leather case.

Amelia's heart dropped into her stomach as Gramps' voice rolled like a penny in the gutter. 'This is something I've had to hide for a very long time. I thought that I could raise you and then die in peace in this city. But now we're in trouble. Big time. They'll be looking for you. You'll end up dead. Dead like your Mama!'

Amelia gawped and sunk to her knees. 'Dead, like Mama? But she died squashed by a bendy bus, Gramps. You said.'

'I lied.' Gramps head fell to his chest. Amelia leant back, awkwardly into the vacuum cleaner.

'All my life's been misery since your Mama died. I've had to live with her death and the knowing that there are people in this city, that would kill you too,' he said looking up. Gramps' hands were shaking as he lit the stub of a cigar. 'I kept the truth of your Mama's magic hidden for a reason, 'Melia. You were not supposed to find it.'

Amelia's life seemed to shrink inwards leaving her as a tiny twitching maggot in the centre. Exposed and alone to circling vultures.
She squeezed her hands together watching a single plume of yellow smoke coiling around Gramps.
'What's it got to do with Mama?' Amelia said. 'I don't understand what you're saying,' she said biting her lip. Her mind whirled with the years of taunts and jokes she'd had that she lived alone with her Gramps. How her mum had been stupid enough to get squashed by a bendy bus on the way back from picking dandelions in a city park.
'We're not the only person in London with a beat-up old telly like that for no good reason, 'Melia. That was your Mama's telly! When they found out your Mama was discovering magical secrets and that she was going to share them, they rubbed her out. Gone. Just like that. Leaving little you with little old me.'
'Little me with little old you?' Amelia said, with a lump growing in her throat. Her face tightened and her fists clenched; feeling this

vulnerable was hard. She wanted to just bolt for the door. Run away. Be done with it all. But it wasn't safe out there either.

Amelia remembered the clanging of the police cars' metal teeth, the insane police officers. She felt in her gut that what Gramps was saying could be true. 'Who was it Gramps? Who killed Mama?' she asked.

'I don't know. I do know that they stole her Wonder, Amelia. Till her beautiful rich black skin went an awful GREY and she was lost and sad every minute of the day. She never fully found her Fantastic Self.'

'Her Wonder?' Amelia clamped her palms to her mouth.

Gramps shuffled closer and opened the case, handing her a tired old envelope. It was pale blue with a drawing of a bluebird singing on a twig.

'For me?' Amelia felt her eyes sting with tears. She unfolded the envelope as though it were the petals of a soft flower.

My Beloved Amelia,

If you are reading this it means that you have discovered that you too hold the key to magic. See your Fantastic Self and the entire Universe will open its arms to you with love and light and magic and Wonder to help you with all you have ever dreamed.

Can you do that, Amelia? Can you dare to be all that you TRULY are in a world that might have forgotten itself? The magic reflection will show you and everyone their Fantastic Selves.

If you are reading this then there is only one person in London who can help you. Take the letter inside this envelope and post it as quick as you can.

I love you more than I can say. When you have your own children one day, you will understand.

X

Amelia looked at the second envelope folded inside. She pulled it out whilst shivering with goosebumps. Her mother? Her mother? Her mother? Her mother! She clutched the letter to her vest. The letter inside the envelope slipped onto the carpet. Amelia read the address on it.

Mister S. Peach Prime Minister of England.
10 Downing Street London. SW1A 2AA

The Prime Minister? Amelia turned her eyes to the ceiling; Susan Strange had been on the phone to the Prime Minister!

She remembered the police's words… 'The Prime Minister of England states in Law 999, that no child may unlawfully enter into divine, magical, mysterious or wondrous experiences.' 'But he wanted Susan Strange to smash the Fantastic Telly! Why would he be able to help?' She looked inside the envelope. A tiny glass vial of ointment with hand writing in ink, the words on it said:

Flimsy Gizzard's Fabulous Grown-Up-Repellant for Amelia
x
Amelia scrunched up her nose and squinted at the label.

'Flimsy Gizzard? What a peculiar name. Amelia wondered who he was and how her mother knew him. He didn't sound like he was from London. But where was anyone called Flimsy Gizzard from? Amelia shrugged it off. She unscrewed the lid and smeared a little on her hand.

Her flesh vanished.

Amelia blinked.

'MAGIC,' she breathed in capital letters. She could see straight through the hole in her hand to reveal the carpet below. 'More magic than the moon at noon!' she gasped. A creaking sound behind them made her start. Amelia turned and scrabbled to her feet, pulling her sleeve over her invisible patch. An old brass telescope had been shoved through their letterbox. A magnified beady eye glared right in at her. Amelia felt a huge flame of injustice ignite in her belly and didn't have time to think about what she was doing. She knew who it was and this time… she was furious about it. The telescope wriggled this way and that to get out of the letterbox.

'Too late!' Amelia yelled and yanked open the door.

Susan Strange fell forwards with a thud into their kitchen. Her weight shook the dishes from the rack. They crashed to the floor. Amelia screeched. It was like a bolt of electricity up her spine.

'This is our flat,' Amelia's cheeks bulged. 'Our telly. And you don't scare me anymore.'

Susan Strange heaved herself up, pulling the door partly from its hinges. Her eyes boggling, she cleared her throat and roared. 'You are nothing more than your mother was, you little squit. A dirty rodent in the building.'

Amelia's face dropped. Her cheeks drained of colour.

'When I came here to watch you, I couldn't wait to pickle you in my shed with all those other filthsome grottbag fluffy bunnies and froggies. You are as I expected, a worm!'

Amelia's new found confidence dropped into her belly and flapped about like a dying fish.

'What do you know about my mother? Why do you want her telly?'

Gramps hobbled over. 'Now listen here missy…' but his voice petered out, staring into the fearsome woman's glare. Susan Strange's laughter made Amelia's hair stand on end. 'I'll be back to get that telly and your wormy squit of a granddaughter too. Don't tell me you ain't often asleep in that chair over there, Granddad. I've seen ya!' She turned and marched out into the hall, slamming the broken door behind her.

A cold silence hung in the room behind her. Amelia stood up feeling Gramps reach out to stop her. But all she could do was grab her Mama's envelope… and run.

Chapter 11

Dark Night of the Soul

Racing along the corridor, Amelia heard the Uglies swarming after her. Her mind whirled with what she had to do, 'got to post the letter, got to post the letter.' How could she get downstairs without Susan Strange seeing her? She wavered, turning her head left and right.

Ding! She had a plan.
Amelia grinned and opened the steel hatch to the laundry chute. It creaked in the dark. The smell of rotten socks, armpits and mouldy cheese hit her. She pinched her nostrils and ushered the Uglies in. They slimed and slobbered along the roof of the chute. Amelia held on tight to the envelope and chucked herself down after them. Squealing with fear, swooshing up and around the entire tunnel, she

exploded out of the iron hatch outside with a crash!

'I'm not a pathetic squit. I'm more than that. I'm more.' She filled with tears racing down the street. Her feet pounding fast across the city. 'I'll show her.

I'll become my most Fantastic Self like Mama didn't finish doing herself… and no-one's gonna stop me.'

The pigeons took off in huge flusters clearing her icy path. The Uglies billowed up ahead of her. They blew through the morning air, a hurricane of shapes against the backdrop of city buildings. Amelia kept an eye out for insane police cars and police officers who could turn the very daylight off.

Clutching her arms to her body for warmth, she ran, checking that there were no weird police about and when she reached the red post box came to a sudden stop. She stood on tippy-toes and lifted the letter up towards the slit. A dark feeling in her heart made her pause. She stared up and into the post-box's dark rectangular hole wondering what it was.

'It would seem that nothing today is as it seems,' she said. 'Should I send this letter from my Mama, to the Prime Minister?' she said out loud.

A cold wind whipped about her ears and howled into the box where it groaned into its depths. Amelia's hand trembled. She didn't
like the feeling here one bit. 'Should I?'
Quick as a city fox, she slung the letter in and...

Wham!

The slit grabbed her hand. Its iron grip made her scream. Amelia tugged left and right to pull her hand away. Its grip held strong. Her hand throbbed with the ice cold pressure of the steel. She wriggled free and pulled herself loose, stumbling backwards. Her skin scratched and bleeding, she stared up in horror. The slit grinned, and as quick as it had come alive, was still and solid again. Her imagination filled with nightmares of London coming to life and gobbling everyone up. She was going to look at her Fantastic reflection in the telly again if it was the last thing that she did. She had to know her Fantastic Self to survive this.

She could NOT be S for Snoozing or B for Bored.

She had to be F for Fantastic.

She made her choice.

Amelia practically flew up the stairs at Chewing Gum Gutters and into Flat Eleventy-Seven. Home had never felt so good. She knew that

she had been feeling worthless when the post-box had tried to eat her hand. She now knew for definite that she should not have sent that letter. Had her feeling rubbish made the post-box horrid? Or was the universe trying to tell her something? The opposite to when the Earth light came in the Shed of Pickled Parts and gave her power to make the ugly things come to beautiful life? Mama felt close and the magic of the universe even closer. She knew exactly what she had to do.

'Graaaaamps!' she yelled, the Uglies tumbling through the corridor behind her. She stood and stared at Flat Eleventy-Seven. Her mouth dropped. The Fantastic Telly was being dragged out of the door by three police officers. Gramps stood with his head bowed, his hands tight on his walking stick. The silhouette of Susan Strange rubbing her hands with glee blocked the window's light. Amelia clocked the bearded television presenter appearing from the stairwell behind her.

'And as fate would have it,' he gestured with over-enthusiastic hands, 'the impassioned Amelia was too late. Too late to stop life's cruel hand dealing her another card...'

'Oh shut up,' Amelia threw over her shoulder at him and lurched towards the police. 'That's mine give it back.'

One of the officers turned and stared down at her. His eyeballs glistened with a purple tinge. 'Oh, contraire Miss Firebrand. We have it by order that this is now the property of the City of London and will be destroyed within the next twenty-four hours'

Twenty-four hours..? But that's only five days away from the Eighth Day! Amelia yelped to herself. I haven't found my Fantastic Self yet, let alone be ready to show all of London.'

Susan Strange called over the din. 'Get out of the way, Squit.'

'No. This is not happening. Do something Gramps,' Amelia said. She'd heard a million people use the phrase, I wanted to tear my hair out...but until this moment she had never

understood what it really meant. Grabbing handfuls of her tight brown curls and tugging so hard that her scalp burned,
Amelia yowled at them. Her face was wild with rage.
The police officers grinned. Each of them had rows of metallic monster teeth. Susan Strange swung by, sending Amelia to the floor with the weight of her hefty bosom.
'Bleaurrgh.' Amelia scrabbled up. The lift doors closed.
The Fantastic Telly, the police and Susan were gone.
Amelia howled with a rage from her gut that made every vein in her face bulge beetroot red. The wind from the open window caught the door of her flat and slammed it in her face. She stood crying and felt an inner bleakness flood her. She yelled at Gramps that he had let her down and ran back into the flat, the Uglies only just making it in time for her to disappear behind her door.
Amelia fell on to her bed and kicked and screamed, her duvet and pillow case flying into the air. She laid breathing, breathing,

and breathing and then an old familiar sensation of nothingness came over her.
It wasn't that she had felt this way forever. But sometimes, when times were tough, a numb nothingness spread through her every cell, like a disease.
Like falling off your bike in the middle of London and no-one wanting to help.
L is for Lonely.
And every inch of her universe echoed with her grief.
Above her on shelves and bookcases the Uglies began to fester. They heaved and sighed until from her heavy eyelids she was sure that they were fading into the plastic of the shelves. The Uglies were no longer robust and plump, but soggy and flat like old lettuce leaves.
Amelia didn't care.
She didn't care about anything anymore.
She sunk into her bed.
Her socks felt suddenly damp.
She could barely be bothered to move her eyeballs the millimetre downwards it would take to see why that was.

When she did, she saw a grey fluff of mould was growing on her socks and a wet mildew was blanketing her mattress. Amelia groaned. Feeling something in her hair, she discovered spiders were lacing cobwebs into her curls.
Amelia could barely breathe.
Her lungs sunk deep into her chest.
Hours passed. The clock yawned through time and space.
Amelia made a super-human effort and reached for a hand mirror on the bedside table. Looking in her reflection she saw her skin had sallowed. Her lips were downturned, her eyes hollow and empty.
Eugh, she was giving up and so was all of life.
The Uglies' original shed-rotting stench filled the room. Amelia groaned again, her lungs filling with the wet of their decay. Utterly helpless her head reeled as to why she could not see her Fantastic Self in any-old-mirror.
And why did her Mama get killed leaving her to work this all out by herself. Around her, the bedroom walls sagged, slumping inwards with an

audible moan. Amelia stared up, her eyelids blinking away tears.

'I'm making some of this stuff happen by what I'm thinking in my head. By what I'm feeling in my heart?'

With a judder, the sinking walls turned black and melting tar glooped across the carpet towards the bed.

From the blackness, gloomy hands reached for her. Over the carpet, up the bedstead, down the pillows, closer, closer, closer... were they going to GET her? Was her time UP?

Everyone thinks I'm ugly, worthless, waste of space, she cried.

Amelia Firebrand's heart gave up.

It was all too much.

Too much. Tooooooo MUCH. Or was it?

A trembling in the walls and beneath the floorboards.

Amelia's eyes opened.

Wa-Womb.

Somewhere deep inside, she felt a shimmer of life.

Wa-Womb.

A sudden flash of her Mama's magical shining eyes in her memory.

MAMA?

Wa-Womb.

The tiny shimmer ignited as flame in Amelia's heart.

Her Mama was HERE.

Her jaw clenched. She sprung up, the moss and cobwebs flying in all directions. She inhaled deep into

her body her feet springing on the mattress.

WA-Whoom! The Earth's heartbeat.

'NO!!!'

The hands kept reaching towards her, the walls moaned and the windows wailed. Her stomach churned. She jumped and star-fished her feet across the bed. The lamplight above her vanished, engulfed in the folding ceiling. She clenched her fists and summoned all the strength in her body.

'NO!' she said again with such force that her eyes bulged from her skull, the walls shook, the windows rattled.

Wa-whoom!

'Get BACK.'

The hands catapulted backwards into the wallpaper and Amelia LIT UP with light and LOVE!

'This is MY life. It doesn't belong to you.'
The room whalloped springing back to its original self. The Uglies tumbled from the shelves, humming themselves awake. Amelia spun on the spot, jumping from the bed. She brushed the cobwebs from her face.

'I am my Fantastic Self,' she realised looking down at her knobbly knees with pride. 'I am more magic than in any storybook. I am my Fantastic Self! Love is the way! No-one can stop us!'

The Uglies buzzed in excitement.

Amelia glared into the eyes of the fluttering Uglies poised for her next move. She felt her feet strong rooted to the ground. She squirmed her toes back and forth on the carpet, wondering what to do next. Pain...gone. Now... something else.

Deep in her body she felt a rumble. The floor of Chewing Gum Gutters trembled low, deep and old.

Amelia lit with a smile.

Wa-Whoom!

The warmth from the Earth flooded her body. She closed her eyes...and KNEW what to do. Like her Mama KNEW what to do.

Amelia dropped a question into her heart.
'How do I get the Fantastic Telly back?'
She waited, listening for the answer. She looked out and up at the sky. A light cleared through the clouds.

Wa-Whoom. At once, a picture appeared in Amelia's mind's eye. Edgar Lily.

Gramps. She had to get to them.

Her feet flew across the carpet as she raced out the door. Finding Gramps huddled in front of the radiator eating Fried Flam Fritters with Sergeant Pepper on his lap, a flurry of words escaped her mouth as she explained what they had to do.

Her Big Love Plan!

She pulled Gramps up and stood him in front of his hat-and-coat mirror in the hall.

Gramps sighed. 'Just an old man, 'Melia. All skinny bones and wrinkly knees. Gummy face long best forgotten.'

'Gramps!' Amelia jumped in front of him. 'I think I know a way to find our Fantastic Selves! If we can find a temporary way into our Fantastic selves we might be able to rescue our Fantastic telly and find our Fantastic Selves for real! I think I can show you, you are the greatest Grandpa there ever was!'

Gramps went a funny shade of brownish-purple. Amelia grabbed a saucepan from the kitchen and reaching up placed it on his head. He made a strange sound that was a bit like a cat slipping on ice.

'Yeeeaaooooaaaawwww. Gerrofff, what're you doing?'

'Showing you your Fantastic Self, Gramps!' Although as she looked at him in the mirror, he didn't look that Fantastic yet. Just a bit bananas, standing with a saucepan on his head. What was it the Fantastic Telly did? It made magic? She raced about the kitchen grabbing strings of onions, broom handles, Magic Twister Magic Mixers, aprons, an old potato sack...until, finally...at last... he was wearing a full mad and magical inventor's outfit.

Magic. She thought she saw him smile.

'I look ridiculous. Like a street tramp that's lost his way,' he said, pulling off the trailing onion strings.

Amelia knew something was missing, and it wasn't something from the outfit. It was something INSIDE him. She closed her eyes for a moment and felt for the warmth in her heart again.

Wa-Whoom! The answer came.

'I think you've got to dance, Gramps!'

'Dance? I haven't danced since nineteen-fifty-eight with your Grandma Padma in the old dance hall down Brixton Way.'

Amelia leapt to his rusty wireless radio on the window sill and flicked it on. The tooty-hooty trombones and scratchy old record playing on Gramps' radio station was one of Amelia's favourite songs. She grabbed his hands and sung loud along with the smooth singing lady.

'Summertime and the living is eaaaaasy. Fish are jumpin' and the cotton is high. Oh, your daddy's rich and your ma is good lookin'. So hush little baby, don't you cry.'

Amelia's legs danced left and right, and it only took a few moments for Gramps to join in.

'Have FUN to find a way in a bit closer to your Fantastic Self!' Amelia spluttered with excitement, spinning round and round on the spot. Her baggy school jumper twirling and looping around her.

Gramps heaved to breathe, a cheesy grin emerging on his face.

Together, their hearts beat. They guffawed and laughed out loud.

'Gramps...' Amelia spluttered, spinning him round. 'LOOK!'

In the wonky mirror hanging in the hall, the howls of their laughter hooted louder, Gramps' reflection shone bright as a star. Amelia looked up at him; his huge beaming love lit every corner of the kitchen.

'Amelia. I do feel right-ol'bloomin marvelous! I reckon I'd need that Fantastic Telly to know for sure, but I think I know what to do for now! We'll get that telly back by tomorrow for sure!'

Where's Edgar Lily?

Day 4

THURSDAY

20th December

Chapter 12

The Magic Telephone Box

Amelia Firebrand sat in her Jammy Biscuit
pyjamas and bright-yellowcrash-hat
and grinned, letting out a huge
sigh of relief. She wiggled her toes.
She was with people she trusted,
maybe for the first time. Ever.
Together, Amelia, Gramps, Sergeant
Pepper and Edgar Lily gazed out
over London.
Everything looked a bit grey and
rubbish to Gramps and Edgar Lily
and they weren't shy of saying it to
Amelia.
'Sometimes it looks like London
has had a giant seagull come along
and dollop its breakfast all over it,'
Gramps grinned. 'But, go on.
Tell us what you see, 'melia.'
Amelia scrabbled to balance on

his armchair headrest, Edgar held on to one of her feet to keep her steady.

Amelia gazed out of the window, her nose squashed sideways to the glass. Tired aeroplanes circled the city to land, dozing up high, their droopy eyes gazed back at her with cynical sighs. An antenna at Canary Wharf sung in a shrill voice about the horrid weather and its wish for an umbrella. An audible groan from the roads carrying trails of traffic trembled through the city. Amelia felt a sort of sideways smile emerge on her lips. She readjusted her bright-yellow-crash-hat.

'It's as though all of London has gone completely fruity,' she whispered to them. 'Imagine, that the things you thought were flat and nothingy, had a personality, a life all of their own.'

She looked round at their puzzled faces. She pointed out a dog that was skateboarding on a giant bone down a hill and an operatic singing ice-cream being eaten by a little girl.

'And that each of them was kind of saying something to me that I sort of knew, but had sort of ignored, well, forever.'

Gramps stood up, proud and took a deep breath. Amelia glowed seeing him as his most Fantastic Self.

'Melia, I can see some of it now,' he said. 'I see that that

statue, Nelson's Column is yawning bored. I see that the River Thames is crying out to be swum in and restored its crystal clear water and happy children swiming alive with fishies for our suppers again.'

'I wish I could see,' Edgar Lily said. 'I have this yuck feeling that I'm invisible most days and that no one can see me. And when I hear you talk about a Fantastic world that's all around us, that I

can't see, it makes me feel sad, like there's something even wronger about me, like it's something that I'm missing.'

Amelia breathed deep, wedging her hands into the folds of her pyjamas.

'But when you say you can feel the Earth's heartbeat,' Edgar said. 'It doesn't matter to me that I can't hear it myself. I know it's true.'

'You will hear it, Edgar. And who knows what else. All I know is that we don't have to live in the dark world, if we open our hearts, all of life is beautiful and here for us. And with the Fantastic telly we can show everyone,' she placed her hand on his shoulder.

'I see you, Edgar Lily. You are the most magnificent friend.'

'Ok,' he grinned. 'How can we help you get the Fantastic Telly back?'

Amelia scanned the forecourt of Chewing Gum Gutters.

The police station stood inbetween London's School for No-Good Children and a twenty-four hour kebab shop. Amelia shivered. Three police cars sat outside, their bonnets of teeth snapped at passers-by. How were they going to get in to the police station without being seen? Amelia felt the answer rise from her within her intuitive guidance.

'The red phone box. The one noone pays any attention to. Let's get down there.'

Amelia got dressed as quick as she could. Sergeant Pepper helped her by tying up one of her trainer laces with his paw.

Amelia led the others down and out across the forecourt. She led them to the tatty old red phone box. Gramps and Edgar Lily walked off and up towards the police station.

Amelia had to be clever.

She never felt clever!

She ran her hands around the rusting red metal. The cloud of Uglies droned around her murmuring

delight at the new adventure. The phone booth didn't seem very alive in Amelia's magic eyes, but she knew it would be somehow.

Everything was!

Fear drizzled through her veins, what if it snapped like the post box? Or worse, munched and tried to eat her like the police car? She put on her best I Am Not Crackers Face and I am Just Standing Outside a Phone Box face and reached up, pulling the door open.

The stench of stale alcohol made her splutter. The Uglies thronged together in to a ball of noise above her head. The telephone box sneezed. Amelia held her nose and tried hard not to touch anything too grimy. She daren't even touch the glass. Tattered stickers for taxi-cabs littered the panes. And muddy dog paw marks splattered the corners.

Amelia cleared her throat, 'erm, hello. Is anyone in?' she said, quite amazed at how tricksy her Polite and Pleasing voice sounded. 'I'm not really talking to a phone box. I've got this plan you see. I need to get my Fantastic Telly back. It's one-in-a-zillion. It was my Mama's. It's got magic in it and... well, we're trying to wake up London so as the Earth's heartbeat will get some life back in it.'

'Well, why didn't you say something sooner?' A kind voice said from somewhere in the phone box. 'Where do we need to go?'

'You're not going to eat me or try and bite?' Amelia asked.

Before the phone booth had a chance to reply, she felt the phone-box wobble and from underneath it two large feet appeared, big and bunioned, like an old city pigeon's. They rose up and started walking them down Pudding Bag Lane.

Amelia marveled as people just moved out of the way as though a walking phone booth were as normal as a cat with whiskers.
Pedestrians shuffled by with their heads down and Amelia felt like the Queen of England.
'Ring ring! Ring ring!' The phone box shrilled to Amelia as she swung around inside the booth, a phone directory almost knocking her out.
'Sssh!' Amelia said, flattening her hair down. 'You'll get me in trouble.'
Through the stickers and greasy fingerprints on the glass, Amelia saw Edgar Lilly sitting outside the police station. He was waving his hands in the air and shouting to passers-by.
'Rights for people in wheelchairs!' he yelled. 'Rollercoasters with wheelchair access! Skis for wheelchairs! Skateboards for wheelchairs!'
Amelia grinned, watching Gramps hobble up to Edgar in a disguise of a wig and glasses.
'What was that, sonny? I reckon you're as mad as they come! Wheelchairs and fun fairs. Ridiculous!'
Amelia watched hordes of greysuited passers-by cram around him to hear more.

'Here, that kid's got pink eyes!' one of them shouted.

'Reckon he's a nutter!' another said.

'White hair too, he looks like one of them animal testing rabbits – someone get him a lipstick!' Edgar Lily shouted even louder.

'They're coming, wheelchairs in space are coming!' His eyeballs strained as though he were about to burst if no-one listened to him.

Amelia shunted forwards a little closer with the phone box. 'Stop, stand still,' she said to the phone box, which dropped down on to its base as if dropping its skirts.

The three police cars sat grumbling in the gutter. One of them chewed on an old Diet Joke can and another bragged about how fast it'd gone that day.

Amelia held her breath. Edgar's shouting was getting louder outside.

Gramps' and the crowd's jeering was even louder.

Amelia watched several police officers' race out of the building towards the crowd. Her heart jumped. It was now or never.

'Walk on!' she urged to the phone box, her nose coming unstuck from its glass. Her heart quickened. The phone box stomped from one leg to the other past the crowd. Amelia held her breath. The police cars! One of them stopped chattering. Its bonnet reared up, its exhaust pipe spluttered to sniff the air with suspicion.

'Down, down!' Amelia snapped.

The phone box did as it was told and shunted on to its base. The Uglies were tense, a waft of

different stinky aromas started to fill the booth. Amelia held her nose and crossed her fingers against the glass and her toes in her sparkly red trainers. Edgar's shouting got louder. The police car swished its headlights left and right; was it Edgar the car could sense or was it picking up on Amelia?

She looked to the entrance of Pudding Bag Police Station. The doors were wide open. There on the wooden reception desk stood the Fantastic Telly! So alone looking! It was utterly wrong to see that it was wrapped in Police Line Do Not Cross tape. Amelia felt the squeeze of the tape around her own belly. Youch. The Fantastic Telly, she had to get it back.

She took a deep breath.

'OK,' she swung round to see if Edgar and Gramps were holding the fort. Yes. Good.

'Right. GO!'

The old red phone box wobbled up, Amelia clonked her head on the glass. 'Come on, go go go!' Amelia blurted, turning to look back at the police cars.

WHOOOMPF!

Amelia and the Uglies hit the roof of the phone box. Amelia's shriek was louder than the crowds'. She cradled her head and looked to see what was happening. But there was not time. The phone box yelped. A police car had gnashed its jaws into the rusty red frame.

'Stand still, stand still, stand still,' Amelia pleaded.

The crowd turned to stare at them.

Amelia ducked down low. The Uglies swarmed up into the corners. The officers raced over, Amelia saw the glint of purple in some of their eyes and winced.

Her life froze. In her mind's eye, she was suddenly five years old getting taunted by some big boys in the playground, and then she was sitting in her Mama's lap, listening to songs about the jubjub bird. She felt very, very small. Sat somewhere between love and loss.

An officer stared aghast at the teeth of his car wrapped round the phone box.

Amelia had to be clever.

She never felt clever!

Something Bad Was Happening with a Capital B. She shut her eyes and concentrated on her breathing.

Wa-Whoom!

Whoosh! A huge thud imploded beneath Amelia.

Wa-Whoom!

The Earth's heart beat whallomped through the ground, sending the crowds, the police, the cars and Amelia flying. She felt the familiar warmth rise through her trainers.

Maybe being clever wasn't what the world needed. Maybe it was FEELING DEEP INTO YOUR HEART.

'Keep still!' she yelled to the phone box in the din.

A light whooshed up and through her body right up to her crown. Amelia jumped a foot in the air. A stream of words suddenly sung from her lips, lighting her like a firework. The words were magic words. Ancient words. Secret words. Words from the light of the Universe!

"*****************'' she sang.

The drains along Pudding Bag Lane rumbled. The crowds looked round in amazement away from the phone box and the crashed car. Spumes of horrid gooky water spewed up from the gutters bursting their gunge in everyone's faces. The public's shrieks echoed for miles.

Amelia urged the booth to move.

'Quick, go! Go! Go!' Wa-Whoom!

The phone box took its chance and waddled from one leg to another to the police station. Amelia wobbled inside, pressing her face to the glass. 'There it is!' She pushed open the door, stepping out on to the tiled floor of the police reception. She beckoned the Uglies closer. They streamed above her dangling their wispy threads. Trilling and chirping they twirled their threads around the Fantastic Telly. They lifted and lowered it into the phone box, its battered wheels dangling above Amelia's head.

Outside the crowd roared like a thousand moody lions. She felt the tug inside; did she need to check on Edgar Lily and Gramps? No, they would have to take care of themselves; it felt even more dangerous to wait for them.

'Chewing Gum Gutters. Quick!' The phone box tried to toddle but its load was heavier now. Amelia felt it struggle. Inside the phone box, she jumped in the air with every step it took on the ground to lighten its load. Outside, the

crowds booed and bayed. The crowds had hotted-up outside. Gramps was fending officers of with his stick, pedestrians covered in sewer gunge wailed and howled their complaints at the duty officers.

Amelia kept leaping. They were half way down Pudding Bag Lane, Amelia's lungs heaving from jumping up and down like a yo-yo, when...

WA-Womb!

Such a boom from the Earth!

There it was.

There it was again. A slow, rhythmic thud. The Earth's pulse sent a WOW through them all in the phone box.

'Wait,' Amelia stopped jumping. She touched her heart with a gentle hand and looked out of the window.

London's School for No- Good Children was right there. It stood cold and boxy in the snow, the big building yawned. Amelia whispered. 'Ssh! I can hear her.'
'Hear who?' the phone box blurted.
'Hear whooooo?' the Uglies hummed.
'The rabbit,' Amelia said in awe.

Day 5

FRIDAY

21st December

Chapter 13

Chicken Karma

Dawn, Amelia Firebrand and the Uglies careered through the door of Flat Eleventy-Seven, Chewing Gum Gutters followed by seven schoolpen chickens, squawking and hungry for food and another carefully wrapped treat. The Fantastic Telly swung above them dangerously. It landed with a DONK! Amelia stopped, crumpling to the carpet. She was utterly exhausted. She kicked off her sparkly red trainers, rubbed her tired eyes and grinned. Opening her satchel, she gazed in. Nestled in an old newspaper snuggled one perfect shiny black rabbit and several newly laid eggs. One yellow egg. One pink egg. One polka-dot egg. One orange egg and one blue egg. The mother rabbit looked up at her.

Its big soft brown eyes sparkled. Amelia crawled over to the sofa and placed her satchel on it, taking care to nestle the rabbit into a cushion. She grinned with excitement. Out the window she saw the old phone box standing as ordinary as ever. Gramps and Edgar Lily were trundling towards the building. Amelia got down from the window.

'We did it!' she said and knelt down. Sergeant Pepper hopped up on to the Fantastic Telly. Amelia unwound the tape releasing its screen, soothing it with her squeaky soft whisper of a voice and gently plugged it back in to the wall. The chickens clucked and squawked to join in. As did the rabbit. Emptying an ice cream tub of crayons, Amelia lined it with lilac loo roll. She rolled the beautiful coloured eggs they had rescued, inside. They had to live! Amelia had never wanted anything so much in all of her life. She placed her hands over the clutch, their warmth merging. She kissed them and tucked them into a pile of fluffy socks in the ice cream tub then hauled Sergeant Pepper up and plonked him on top of the nest. His belly bulged over the sides. 'You'll have to sit on the eggs for now. The rabbit's not looking so good,' she said peering over at the shivering rabbit, which sneezed and clucked in the corner. She sat him on her lap and warmed him with a hairdryer, rubbing his black fur with yesterday's school socks. She hauled down her books and cut out a photo of a rabbit. She pasted the photo onto the front of her brightyellow-crash-hat.

'You see. You're a rabbit. Like this one.' Amelia pointed at her head.

Circles of light reflected in the rabbit's eyes.

Amelia stroked his velvet-soft fur, feeling his heartbeat quiver beneath his ribs. She wrapped him in her dressing gown and put him beside her on the sofa.

She pressed her palm to her heart and listened deep. Her feeling was that they needed to get the Fantastic Telly back on and see what was what!

But the telly had other ideas.

'What's wrong with it?' Amelia cried. She turned to look at the swarm of creatures behind her, aghast. Her hands fumbled for a button, a switch, an anything she might have missed. Anger fueled her fire. She sighed exasperated.

'No! You can't not work. What do I do?' Amelia felt her joy about the eggs and the rabbit drain away and the familiar feeling of falling into nothingness take the ground from beneath her. She cradled her head in her hands. But if it doesn't work, then, then...? She looked down at her arms; a grey tinge was seeping through her usual warm-brown tones.
A tap-tapping sound pricked her ears. Sergeant Pepper was springing down from the eggs. A crack zigzagged its way across the blue egg's shell. Amelia lay down and rested her head on the carpet next to the plastic tub. Her body felt smaller and smaller. A tiny blue bald bird stretched its neck out of its shell for the first time. The chick opened its eyes. They were large and round. It squawked as though someone were pinching its beak.
'It doesn't look like a normal bird.' Amelia tried to forget about the telly. She rubbed her own eyes. Its eyes were too big and its body was too small. And it had furry rabbit's

feet and blue downy feathers! Amelia scooped the warm
shell in her hand. 'You don't look like a rabbit either. More like you're just made of magic.' She turned the other half of the shell on its side. She looked down at the chick. It chirped so hard its eyes bulged. Its neck stretched up towards the eggshell in her hand. 'Did you want to keep it?' she said looking at the curious soft blues of the shell.
It scrunched its head into its neck like an old vulture.
'I'll put it down.' Amelia placed the shell back in the tub. The chick scrambled out of the ice cream tub and over to the blue eggshell, its scrawny body trailing with the lilac loo roll. It peered into the first half of the shell, and then into the other. It pecked and tugged and pulled as though it had found a wormy treat. Sergeant Pepper turned up his nose. The chick stepped out from the shell dragging with it a soggy white something.
'Pweep, pweep, pweep.' It dropped it at her knee and looked up at Amelia with calm eyes. It was a damp, folded piece of paper.

The chick jumped up and down on the spot. Amelia unfolded the
paper, which was like the petals of a soggy flower. She scrunched up her nose and concentrated. There were words written on it.
'Sergeant Pepper, the lights.'
'Reow!' He leapt up to the light switch, hitting it with his paw.
The room filled with light. The words on the paper sparked and fizzed with twinkles...

One Human SOUL Life
Amelia Firebrand
Open-Return-Ticket

Amelia scrambled up from the carpet and held the wet piece of paper directly underneath a lamp light on her desk.
'That's me, this is my name!'
There were more words on the ticket. The chick hopped to the carpet. Amelia's heart thudded. The chick ran round in circles. Sergeant Pepper watched the chick and opened his mouth wide. Amelia tapped Sergeant Pepper on the nose. 'No. The chick isn't dinner.' Her

emerald green eyes sparkled. The chick bounced from one of her scuffed trainers to the other.
'Pweeeeep.'
'Oh, I don't speak chicken,' she said.
The chick did star jumps across the floor. Amelia stared up at the ceiling. If a rabbit can be brought up by chickens and not know it is a rabbit, even when shown another rabbit – then what about children? All children were something completely amazing and had come here to be something wonderful. And now, well, now... 'Maybe it's not just me that feels like a rabbit in among the chickens. Maybe lots of children feel this way, just like Edgar Lily shared.'
A tear rolled down her cheek. The chick pweeped up at her, and Amelia fastened her crash-hat strap tighter.
'We got to tell all the children, in case they forgot, that they're A for Amazing! '
The sound of gentle pecking made her turn. To her astonishment, she saw that the pink egg was hatching. The perfect yellow beak of a pink feathered chick emerged. Its eyes were squeezed shut. Amelia's heart fluttered.

'The first time it's seen the earth,' she said in awe, her eyes filling up with tiny pools of salty of water.

She crawled down closer, holding the bulging Sergeant Pepper in her arms. The orange egg hatched next with a sherbet-orange downy soft chick. It stepped on to the carpet with tiny silvery soft rabbit paws. Amelia welcomed the chick stroking its tail with her fingertip. Soon, all the eggs had hatched. The room was now full of the music of cheeping chicks, with pink, yellow, orange and blue fluffy feathers. The Uglies swung above them honking and hooting their hellos.

'Welcome to the world, little ones,' Amelia said.

Amelia sat watching them all realising that she had never felt so happy in all of her life.

Wa-Whoom, the flat trembled.

That's it then. It's all true,' Amelia grinned. 'We got to tell all the children.' She looked over at the clock. It was just gone eight o'clock in the morning; the postman would have been by now too. She had to check for a reply from the letter she sent to the Prime Minister.

The magic letter bringing her special assistance...?

The lift doors closed on Amelia, embalming her in the familiar rotten elevator's stench of stale urine and Barf's Beer.

Through the lift's emergency speaker system, the bearded nature presenter's voice echoed in Amelia's ears.

'And this cold, down-trodden and lonely child, finds a way to bring magic to this aching part of her life with the idea that someone, anyone might be able to help.' A trumpeting fanfare accompanied his announcement.

Amelia stared at the speaker. Was he right? Was she that naive?

A siren wailed in the distance and Amelia shuddered at the thought of the purple police. What if they came again but this time stole the Fantastic Telly? Should she have hid it? Something inside her crumpled. She took a big breath.

Ding! She stepped out of the lift. There was no time to get all thinky about it! Walking past an open door, Amelia waved at old Mrs

Dribbles in Flat One and a Half Point Three. She sat huddled in an armchair watching the news.

'Morning, Deary,' Mrs Dribbles called.

Amelia walked across to the rows of locked letter boxes, a number on each one for each flat. She unlocked Flat Eleventy-Seven's and peered inside. There in the dust on top of a pile of aged envelopes for the previous tenants and a flyer for Bucket-O-Chips, the local chippy, laid a pristine white envelope. Typed! With Amelia's whole name on.

Amelia's heart jumped. She grabbed the envelope and tore it open. Her hands shook. The letter inside had been typed too, but her names had been filled in - in biro – and filled in wrong!

Dear Miss/Mr/Mrs ALAN Firebrand,
Thank you for your letter dated somewhere sometime lately. Your letter is very important to us.

We are sorry that we are unable to reply to you personally, it is our aim to reply to each letter sent, but not necessarily to read it.

Signed on behalf,

Sebastian Peach

The Prime Minister of All of England

His signature had been stamped in green ink. Amelia stared at the letter. 'I can't believe they even got my name wrong! How rude.' With Fantastic magic burning in her eyes she knew what the letter really said:

You are a silly little girl and we are not interested in your letter.

That's it? She gawped. That's the reply to my Mama's special letter? Why didn't the Prime Minister want to help her? Why did Mama think he would? Amelia remembered the police citing the law again, the Prime Minister of England states in Law 999, that no child may unlawfully enter into magical, mysterious or wondrous experiences.

'Mama thinks the Prime Minister is someone he's not, she realised. 'Maybe he was different when Mama was alive? Did he give her the telly?'

Amelia stared up at a drip, drip, dripping from the peeling ceiling and back down at the letter as a yellow drop of water landed on her letter with a splosh. A familiar feeling in her belly, a sinking sensation of nothing ever going right rose to the surface. Never, never, always things were rubbish and she just knew it and was so fed up with it. She took a deep breath and a soft tingle in her stomach warmed her.

She stared. Feeling. Listening. Watching. The name on the letter swirled in a mist of words and the words rearranged themselves:
Signed on behalf of
Sebastian Peach ... The Prime MONSTER!
The letter box door slammed shut with a clang. Its key fell to the floor. Amelia gasped and dropped the letter. Suddenly the sound of Mrs Dribble's telly went up very loud.

Too loud. Amelia turned round.

Mrs Dribble sat still, knitting a toy cat, blissfully unaware. Amelia covered her ears and stared. The voice of a newsreader reporting   from outside Big Ben boomed into the hallway. The Prime Minister was on the telly.

Coincidence? Wa-Womb! Amelia didn't think so!

The Prime Minister stood stooped, his ice-cream cone of yellow hair pointing high. Amelia crept closer to Mrs Dribble's door and peered to see better. The light from the telly in the dark flat danced on her cheeks.
Amelia blinked hard. That's him. The one I wrote too. The Prime Minister, his grey suit, grey trousers and waffling long sentences, blurred and reformed. With her magical insight Amelia saw the Prime Monster's eyes darken. There was a flash!
A flash of purple. A flash of brilliant white. And a hypnotic swirl. His suit flashed neon orange and green.
'Oh these prats in suits,' Amelia heard Mrs. Dribble mutter.
Unknown to Mrs. Dribble and the newsreader, Sebastian Peach, the Prime Monster laughed and cackled, turned round, pulled down his trousers and mooned the cameras. Amelia watched and listened with her Fantastic knowing.
'Brain Drain Plans!' he cried.
'Children of London's WONDER to be Stolen. On Christmas Day. THE Most Boring Moment of the Year for Children – The Queen's Speech. 3pm.

ALL of LONDON will fall into a DEEEEEP SLEEEEEP.' Amelia repressed a shriek. Mrs. Dribble reached for a Rich Tea biscuit. 'Na-na-na-na-na!' the Prime Monster guffawed.

A member of the public handed him their newborn baby wrapped in soft blankets. The Prime Monster's wicked eyes glinted.

He held the baby, cooing like a pigeon for a moment and then handed the baby back to its parents. Not being able to see what was happening, the parents looked on with pleasant smiles into the camera.

Amelia gawped. The baby squealed and shrieked, its skin had turned fish paste GREY! Like so many children she had seen in London! So this is what the Fantastic Telly meant, that she had seven days to discover her Fantastic Self and eight days to show all of London.

She counted again on her fingers; there were just THREE days to go.

Amelia stood in shock. Wave after wave of realisation hit her. Is the Prime Monster the man that killed her Mama? Did he Brain Drain her Wonder too? Her own brain whirred with the pain of everything she had discovered.

Amelia Firebrand cycled down Donkey Butter Street dodging prams, cars and London buses. She screeched up Pudding Bag Lane towards the Pudding Bag Lane tube station. In the basket, Sergeant Pepper scrunched his eyes up in the sleet. Like a pilot's scarf the rabbit's ears flapped behind him. The blue chick perched on the handlebars, wrapped in a sock and wearing its egg shell for a hat. Its bunny feet nestled in the two halves of its eggshell. Together, they skidded past hordes of commuters. A man as glum as gluepots swooshed a newspaper at Amelia, spilling his coffee.
'Shouldn't you be at school?' he said.
'Been there, done that!' Amelia yelled back. She stood up from the saddle and pedaled in the direction of the Royal Bank of Truffle and Snout and the Houses of Parliament. Children watched her from the back seats of cars. She realised that every single one of them had faces just as grey as that baby's. The headquarters of the Royal Bank of Truffle and Snout gleamed in the snow. Amelia stared through its windows. Behind slatted blinds, grown-ups sat at computers chewing on

paper clips and glugging coffee from foam cups.

'What do you think they do in there all day?' Amelia said.

Sergeant Pepper shrugged.

Amelia leant her bike against the wall, put it on its stand and pulled a can of green spray paint from her pocket. She stepped up onto the pavement and tipped her head back.

N is definitely for Naughty, she said. She had that feeling that she defiantly was not B for Behaving. And it felt very good!

The high-rise offices towered over her. The nozzle was stiff. She squeezed it with the tip of her finger. A hiss of paint sprayed outwards. 'Bum,' she said. The paint trailed down her arm, down her knee and onto the pavement. She stepped up close to the vast windows of Truffle and Snout, shook the can again and then wrote across the glass in letters as large as herself...

Wake up, London!

See Your Fantastic Self

The excitement was almost unbearable.

Wa-Womb! The Earth's heartbeat in unison with Amelia's.

She had never done anything so naughty in all of her life. What would Gramps do? What would Mrs Chump say? She stepped back.

'Uh-oh,' she turned to see trouble on its way. Why did she never get away with anything! she wondered.

Through the glass startled faces looked up at her. The fluorescent strip lights reflected yellowishgreen against their skin. Amelia heard a jangle of keys. 'Double bum.'

A security guard rounded the corner. 'Oi, come 'ere. What do you fink you're doing?' he said. Amelia stood on the spot. Sergeant Pepper hissed from the basket. The rabbit snuffled deeper inside it and the blue chick leapt up and down, tweeting.

'I'm trying to help,' she said.

'Help? Help what? That'll take me days to get off, you little maggot. I'll inform the police right now. I've got a button, a special button.'

'Press your button. I'm here because it's, well, it's important,' she said, with her hands on her hips.

'Right that's it. I'm pressing my button.'

Crowds of workers pressed their noses to the glass from inside the office.

'We've got their attention now, you three.' Amelia pulled out of the basket a folding-stool and one of Gramps' hearing trumpets. She stepped onto the stool and cleared her throat.

'Grown-ups of London,' she called through the back-to-front hearing trumpet.

Their faces scowled at her through the glass. Their heads shook. The swing doors opened and bemused workers walked out onto the street, pulling on their jackets and lighting cigarettes.   'I've found a way we can be! All of the Universe is ALIVE the earth wants to BREATHE! Life wants us to be free! There is a magic mirror! Look! A Fantastic Television and if you look in it you see your Fantastic Self and, AND... The heartbeat beneath London is EXHAUSTED and it needs us to all start laughing and dancing and, er, well... being loving again and to come back to life!'

'What? What's she on about?' the grown-ups jeered the same way Amelia's class had. She juddered inside and took a deep breath.

'There's gonna be a MASSIVE BRAIN DRAIN on Christmas Day! All of the Wonder in your children's hearts is going to be stolen and you'll all fall into a terrible deep SLEEP! You won't wake up!' she waved her hands in the air.

'Fantastic Telly? City asleep? Who are you, Sleeping Beauty?' a man guffawed.

'What? My life is blimmin' Fantastic,' a man eating a donut said.

'If we don't stop the Prime Monster,' Amelia cried, 'it'll be too late and all the children will turn to sleepy sludge!'

'Well, how's that then?' the crowd said. 'She can't even pronounce Minister correct!'

'If everyone looked in the
Fantastic Telly they'd see a way to stop this!' Amelia cried. Don't watch TV….Look at your reflection in it instead!

'What an odd kid. What a loony. And look she's got a cat! And a rabbit! And a bird! Heh, she must've painted it blue!' 'A cat! I'm allergic.'

'A rabbit! I'm hungry.'

'We don't need the Prime Monster and schools and stuff! It's clogging us up and making us GREY! The Earth beneath London is ALIVE! If we listen to it, we can make our own magic city!'

A hotdog vendor pulled up in his van and slung a net out of the window, swiping at Sergeant Pepper, the chick and the rabbit. They hopped and squawked to escape him.

Amelia scowled and spanked the vendor's hand with the hearing trumpet. She looked at all the office workers. Their complexions now the colour of freshly laid paving slabs.

'If only you would look in my Fantastic Telly,' she pleaded. 'I've got a London Underground, tube ticket, you can all use it to get to mine and go and have a look!'

The workers laughed, holding their bellies they howled with laughter and trailed back inside the building.

Amelia slumped to the pavement. She ran her hands over the ground. Thin weeds poked up and through the paving slabs. She felt the softness of all her love and hope and dreams wave through her being.

And, immediately...

Wa-Womb.

There it was.

There it was again. A sad, slow rhythmic thud. You're dying, Amelia cried. We all are.

'Nothing I do is working!!' Amelia stamped. Her world crumbled. 'Tomorrow, I'm gonna find this Prime Monster and see what is really going on!'

Day 6

SATURDAY

22nd December

Chapter 14

The Wonder Crusher

Amelia pulled herself out of
bed and stretched her arms up
towards the ceiling. Today I am my
Fantastic Self.
In the night, she had had a dream
that told her exactly what to do.
Amelia felt that the ONLY way she
could be TRULY CLEVER was by
listening to her deepest self.
Noone else. No matter what they said.
She rubbed her hands together with glee,
'I'm gonna be my most
Fantastic self
and listen to the beautiful
Universe in my heart!'
It was time to be brave and clever… Amelia
Firebrand never felt brave and clever! Was it
possible to find a way into the Houses of
Parliament?

It was time to call in her Mama's support. She smothered herself in her Mama's Grown-Up Repellent. The effect was instant – she vanished. Only her bright-yellowcrash-hat hovered in the mirror. Amelia wheeled through the crowds of Christmas shoppers on her bicycle. They fell like skittles out of her way.

The Houses of Parliament stood towering above her. Tiptoeing into the main entrance, through scores of Japanese tourists, Amelia ran, jumped and cleared a Welcome Attendant, knocking his cap flying. She heard the confused shouts of people she was knocking out of the way. But she had to get to the Prime Monster! She clutched her chest, imagining that Gramps and Edgar Lily were close with her.

Inside, the Houses of Parliament were just as she had imagined. Grown-ups grumbling in a tower of ornate buildings. Amelia tried to block them out. Their hearts plopped in their chests like splats on the pavement. The braying politicians parted from her as easily as the commuters had.

Amelia explored chamber after chamber of oak-paneled rooms, stepping soft across the carpet pile. How she got to the heart of the building, she was unsure. The magic inside of her heart was guiding her and was seeming more natural than ever.

Feeling her flushed cheeks melting the Grown-Up Repellent, she smudged some more on her cheeks. She followed a long line of politicians crowding through a grand doorway. She wove between saggy bottomed suits and nylon beige tights. A camera from Breakfast Yawn TV was being set up.

  Amelia looked straight into the lens and realised that this was the room that was always on the news.

'Order! Order!' A voice boomed from a wooden plinth at the front of the room.

She looked around at the rows of wooden seats encased in green leather. 'It's the House of Commons!' she realised. Amelia scuttled behind the flock of people, ducking down beneath a bench. From her hiding place, she was aghast to see the Prime Monster being shimmied into the room by a bunch of drooling aids. Amelia shivered in her anorak. Why oh why would he be the one my Mama thought could help me? As he walked past in his squeaky-clean, ultra-ironed suit, the Prime Monster's large nostrils sucked up the air around him.

Amelia held her breath – as if that was going to make a difference! He strode passed and she suppressed a snort. Emblazoned on his buttocks he had daubed a large red, white and blue bull's eye board. He was as weird as a crocodile on a sun-lounger! She scuttled out behind the other men to find a better hiding place and

saw a wooden plinth at the front. She ducked behind it and crouched beside Madam Speaker's ankles, which rolled over the sides of her patent leather shoes.

'My Right Honourable Friends,' she heard the Prime Monster bray. 'It is my pleasure to announce today that great wads of cash are being made by our nation! What a wonderful place to be!' His icecream slick of yellow hair and greasy porcelain skin made her feel sick.

She hugged her knees to her stomach.

'Great people. Today is a day that is not tomorrow, nor yesterday, but something entirely different!'

Amelia huffed and slumped against the wooden paneling. Something poked from the wood into her back. A small door handle... and a tiny wooden door. Just tall enough for her to fit through.

'I bet that's it!' She turned the brass handle and pushed the door out and open into a red carpeted tunnel. An engraved plaque in the wall read:

Head Quarters - The Royal Bank of Truffle & Snout.

There was something rotten about it, like musty goat's milk and old socks covered in shiny stuff.

She pulled the door to and crept along and out into a cavernous, glass-domed room. The rabble of the politicians hushed. Staggering backwards into a golden statue of the Prime Monster, she saw that he held a fan of fresh banknotes. Weird.

Amelia stepped off the red carpet and on to the black and white ceramic tiles. Diamond-encrusted spikes shot up through the tiles and barred her way. Droplets of diamond loops dangled from crystal birds standing in plastic trees. Pink flamingos paraded in front of the tall veranda windows in front of her, overlooking the Thames. Wide chaise lounges stood with massive lion's paws.

'They're real,' Amelia shuddered at the claws sticking out from them. 'What is this place? And what's that?'

Amelia heard the sound of footsteps from behind an enormous panelled door, which pattered to a stop. The great big door opened. Amelia ducked! The corridor filled with a black shadow. Amelia pulled her arms and legs close to her body. A handful of grey suited men and women streamed in through the door to form an orderly line, followed by the Prime Monster.

Sebastian Peach was burping a tune to himself. 'Get out of my space,' he belched to his aids. 'I've got thinking to do.' He curled a finger round a twirl of his groomed yellow roller-coaster hair-do and positioned himself in the throne.

Behind it, Amelia curled her head and shoulders into her lap. She heard him wrenching and cracking his knuckles, and then he bit down on them hard. She peeked up to see an arc of feet in tight shoes circling him.

'Right. Tactical meeting you loathsome idiots. We've got some trouble here! SOMEONE. A very particular young girrrrl, in fact,' he rolled the R in his mouth for a moment, 'has found her way in to The Fantastic Borderland of Things.

Amelia peeked her head out to see him pull a photograph out of his left lapel. He glared at it with huge bug eyes.

'This girl, she's the TARGET! I have the photo to prove it. She has got to go. Not only is she very particular,' the Prime Monster continued, 'she can see EVERYTHING and must be stopped or else she'll be blabbing to everyone out there about how awful their lives are and how great mine... I mean ours, is.'

'But, Sir? Who is she? How will we find her? Is she in the phone book?'

'Arrrgh. You idiots. What are we ruling the world for if we can't find one ugly kid from a cowpat of a high-rise council estate in this rotten city?'

Amelia's heart dropped into her stomach with a thud.

'Is he talking about me?'

'I want all the Wonder squeezed out of every child in the UK by Christmas Day. That includes squeezing it out of this little BRAT!'

Amelia shivered. Her magical knowing had been right.

Amelia saw behind the grown-ups heads another door leading from the main room. A sign on it said:

The Wonder Crusher

Amelia gasped. 'So that's it!'

One. Two. Three. Four. She held her breath and crawled along behind them to the door. She turned the doorknob. The door opened with a soft squeak. She crept inside. A long velvet-red corridor led to a room that bustled with noise and activity. She closed the door behind her and crept along towards it. A moaning wail filled the cavernous glass room.

Amelia stared up at an enormous translucent plastic machine. It reached to the domed roof. Millions of what looked like twirling plastic tubes led from somewhere outside the building and in and down into the machine. A large pump wheezed and spluttered with such a commotion that Amelia had to hold on to her ears. She walked around the machine in a gruesome sort of awe and read the huge flashing sign of brightly lit bulbs in arrows and neon flashing lights above the Wonder Crusher. Children's Wonder IN HERE!

Amelia stumbled back in shock, clutching her chest. So this was it. She stood as tall as she could,

and taking an enormous breath walked inside. Children's Wonder oozed through the tubes in an array of pulsing pinks, lemon yellows and silver brights. Men and women in grey suits with clipboards walked around stroking their chins and taking measurements from the straws. Amelia ducked behind a drinks machine and watched, realising what the Prime Monster, Sebastian Peach had been doing. A giant switchboard showed her that every tube led to a school desk, telly or computer in every building in the city. Slowly sucking away the children's Wonder, when the children would just be going about their normal day. A siren bellowed from a speakerphone above her head.

She jumped up. The siren seemed to signal the end of the working day. Amelia watched all the grown-ups leave. They closed the doors behind them.

She clambered out. Seeing everyone had gone, Amelia walked around the machine. She brushed her hand along its side. She pressed her ear to it and heard a wheezing, troubled heart. It was sad too. Amelia patted its plastic sides and gazed into the Wonder of London's Children for the first time. Tears rolled down Amelia's cheeks.

'What do they want our Wonder for, why would they keep it? Grownups wouldn't be interested in our Wonder.'

The moon rose over the Thames, brightening Amelia's view through the floor to ceiling windows. A blade twirled in an enormous vat. The children's Wonder mixed into a beautiful bright swirl of pinks, yellows and greens. Psychedelic custard.

Amelia squinted at the Wonder's bright light. Its golden brilliance washed over her. It delighted her ears with a low hum. She wanted to dive into it. Dive in and swim forever. Amelia's toes tingled. Her feet walked her

closer to the vat. She inhaled a deep breath. The Wonder's sweet scent of summer apples, ripe-red raspberries and fields of corn lifted her into the air. She swayed and her feet dangled beneath her. She shook herself.
Wake Up Amelia!
She collapsed to the ground. Amelia shook herself to, and got up. She followed the edge of the Wonder Crusher into the next room. Machines whizzed with the Wonder and reams of green paper. 'So they're making paper with our Wonder?' she said.
'Why? I don't get it.' She raced alongside the whirring conveyor belts. Then stopped, stunned. The Queen of England's head rolled in front of her eyes thousands of times.
'MONEY! Money..?' Amelia gasped.
'That's it! They're making money out of our light our magic!'
Amelia felt sick. She held on to her stomach. Thousands more banknotes churned past her. 'I have to get out of here.'
Amelia raced back to Chewing Gum Gutters, pacing on the tube, biting her fingernails on the escalators, leaping through the barriers at Pudding Bag Lane. By the time she got back

and into Flat EleventySeven she thought she was going to have an asthma attack. Her lungs throbbed with exhaustion.

The front door was open. Amelia screeched to a halt. The sitting room blurred with chaos and noise. Susan Strange blocked the light from the window! Edgar Lily cowered beneath her. The Uglies zipped and
zapped, storming through the space. The Fantastic Telly sat shivering centimetres
     beneath Susan's gleaming hatchet.

Amelia froze lollipop cold.

'Oh no, I should have hidden it!' Gramps was nowhere to be seen.

Susan Strange walloped her son out of the way. He flew backwards, his chair twanging into the radiator. 'More brain cells in a Satsuma,' Susan yelled, lurching forwards to the telly. 'What are you all doing?'

Amelia and Edgar scarpered away and cowered in the corner small as mice.

'Gimme that!' Susan bent down to the telly. Amelia winced from the corner, staring directly into Susan's rumpsome buttocks. Susan thumped the television and sneered.

'It doesn't even work! It's the biggest joke there is. There's nothing to be scared of after all.' She turned to see Amelia.
'She's back!' Susan Strange's eyes boggled, one eye glaring down at Amelia, the other at the door. 'Now gimme back my Pickled Parts. I'm hungry for me tea.'
The Uglies screeched a high pitched and wailing, 'Nooooo!'
'You horrid grotsomes. You are so hideous and ugly!' Susan Strange hollered.
Amelia Firebrand cowered like the rabbit in the school cage, remembering Mrs Chump as a giant cockle-doodle-doo. Beneath Susan Strange's huge shadow, Amelia felt a gentle vibration beneath the floorboards.
Wa-Whoom.
There it was.
There it was again. Amelia breathed deep and allowed the surge of warmth to move up from the Earth and through the building. Amelia absorbed every drop of the Earth's LOVE and opened her eyes.
The room froze in time and space.
Amelia held her breath tight. Susan Strange dropped on to her knees and looked into the

Fantastic Telly. The world seemed to stop. The high-pitch of the odd dog yapping in other flats, dropped to gruff rumbles. The sound of cars in the night honking outside softened to a distant drone.
The Fantastic Telly crackled with noise. Wa-Womb! The Earth's heartbeat whispered. Amelia, Edgar and all the creatures leaned in closer. In the first few seconds, Susan Strange's reflection looked the same to Amelia – gruff, with her monobrow zigzagging from her frown. In the blink of an eye her Fantastic Self bloomed into view.
Her limp hair, which normally clung to her face with grease and speckles of dandruff, flourished with sprouts of long green grasses. Next, elegant stalks of wild flowers sprung from her scalp, her clothes vanished and in their place a dress of dewdrops rose around her and enveloped her being in a magical pearly mist. A light shone from her eyes with such an intensely bright blue that Amelia and the others had to shield their own eyes.
Susan Strange dropped to her hands, an enormous wave of grief spilling from her body.

'I only stole the telly, 'cos I couldn't bear it if someone like your mother lived here again,' she said.

Amelia's eyes stung with the pain in her heart.

'We can't all be running round full of magic and wonder and blimmin' lovely lollipops!' Susan Strange yowled.

'And, this bloke, well, he was something to do with the Prime Minister, well he just found me you see, asked me to get rid of it. Loads of money for me you see. Brought me-self that shed and a new wheelchair for Edgar.'

Amelia felt the pang of truth in her words. The hatred and fear she had of Susan melted from her down into the ground. Amelia and the creatures crept closer and wrapped their arms, tails, snouts, wings and trotters around Susan Strange. The tighter they hugged and cocooned her, the stronger her sparkling river of tears flowed in the reflection.

Amelia just hugged and hugged Susan deeper. It wasn't anger she felt, she felt a sigh of relief in her body.

'Mum, are you OK?' Edgar Lily leant in close.

'I had to kill all the bunnies and squirrels and pigeons in London, they were too blimmin' happy!'

Amelia watched Susan look up at her son and reached out for him to come closer. He fell into her arms.

'Look at you!' she laughed, 'I feel like I've never even seen's ya's! You are more special than I ever dared to see.'

Amelia stared with unblinking eyes. She could hardly believe it. Her mind was saying, No. What? It Can't Happen Like That. But her heart knew. But It Just Did. I Saw It with My Own eyes. She had a sudden, unexpected Fantastic vision!

'Edgar can you get the Fantastic telly to London's School for NoGood Children? Show them their Fantastic selves?'

Edgar grinned. 'Consider it done.'

There was nothing N for Normal about it, Amelia grinned.

And it felt FANTASTIC.

Chapter 15

The Love Machine

Gramps whooped into the room. Amelia's heart jumped for joy. She watched Gramps run over to the bed in a weird way, the way someone who has sat-in-a-chair-all-their-livesway. His back was armchair shaped and his legs permanently bent.
A halo of light from the bulb above the bed reflected back at her from his balding brown crown.
'Help me move this,' he said doing a jig by the bed. 'I've been busy, 'Melia. That Fantastic Telly of yours showed me something seven years ago, after your Mama died, that I was supposed to do.'
He yanked open the wardrobe to reveal something huge inside it. Like a jack-in-the-box a clunking, bunking, dunking, funking machine automatically folded outwards and into the room. It was so big it blocked the light

from the window. Amelia was squidged to the wall by it. Gramps waved his hands in the air.

'I did it, Amelia. I made something magic for us listening to my Fantastic Self!'

Amelia looked at the name carved in the machine's base...

The Love Machine

Amelia clapped her hands and jumped round full circle on the spot. She watched Gramps flick a switch on the contraption. It put itself together in a jig-sawing whirl of lights and colour.

'So, what is it?' Amelia pushed the rubbery contraption away from her and pushed her way around to the only patch of standing room left. Gramps looked up at it with wonder. She had never seen him with such an expression before. It must do something great. It was so beautiful to see him happy. She gave his skinny waist a big hug.

'Ooo-ar, gerrof,' Gramps laughed. 'Let me show you what it does. Run out there for me. Get me the most horrid thing you can find.'

'Horrid? Horrid like sewer goo?'

'No, something useless...'

There was so much gumpf in the flat to choose from. She emptied vases of dust-covered plastic sunflowers and stuffed them in her anorak pockets. Under the phone table in the hall, she found a stack of magazines with photos of people sunbathing on the cover. She stuffed those under her arms. In the kitchen she found seven packs of Grubs Up Granny! pre-made ready food. She carried them all carefully back along the corridor.

From inside the room, Amelia heard Gramps laughing. A glorious deep laugh. It was like a dream come true! It made her grin. She had not heard him laugh in all of her life. Seeing his Fantastic Self was the best medicine. She walked in with the mountain of stuff.

'Here Gramps...' she said.

'Wondercluck! Superbump!' He clambered up a ladder. A funnel in the top of the contraption hummed.

'Pass me the useless gumpf! And watch the miracle of the Love Machine!'

Amelia handed them up to Gramps who wobbled from one leg on the ladder. She watched the plastic flowers fly up high. From the Love

Machine's funnel a long curling pink tongue flicked out like a hungry frog and caught the flowers with a sticky lick.

Before Amelia could blink, they had disappeared.

'Wow. It's alive?' asked Amelia.

'But that means... that means...'

'That's right... it's Fantastic. It's a FANTASTIC model of an old bin system from out the back of Chewing Gum Gutters,' Gramps grinned.

'But how do you know how to create it?'

'You're not the only one with secrets, 'Melia. Your Mama tried to show me an awful lot all them years ago. I've connected to my Fantastic self a few times here and there to know how it works. Listen to me heart, and off we go! And now, look where we are. If only I'd listened years ago.' Gramps leapt back and forth hurling the useless gumpf into the machine.

'Now, get your butt down there, no... there. Open the trap door.'

Amelia pulled a latch and an airfilled bouncing slide yawned out and on to the carpet. A hiss of air blew her back.

'What's it doing?' she yelled.

The Love Machine belched. Down the slide the naff magazines rolled out as a log of oak covered in burping bright green tree frogs. The plastic flowers flew out as fresh rose petals and buds. Amelia danced beneath their petals catching them in her hands. The Grubs-Up-Granny! pre-made food slid out on wooden plates as home-cooked honey-glazed roast chicken and rhubarb crumble and custard.

'Gramps, we have to get this into the City. We've only got twentyfour hours to go! There's going to be a massive Brain Drain on Christmas Day at 3pm, during the Queen's speech – the most boring moment of the year. The Prime Monster's going to take all the children's Wonder and send the rest of London in to a DEEP SLEEP. We've got to stop him!'

'Amelia, hold your holla, let's settle in for the night with Sergeant Pepper and that funny chick, and eat this yummsome grub!' Gramps smiled.

Amelia reached out her hand to his.

It would be their first meal together, she realised with a smile.

Day 7

SUNDAY

24th December

Christmas Eve

Chapter 16

The Great Cloud Batter

Amelia's alarm clock trilled Jingle Bells to wake her up.
Amelia shuffled herself out of bed, and lobbed the alarm clock at the wall. It imploded into tiny cogs with a thwang! She tugged on yesterday's socks and last week's as yet, unwashed jeans.
Amelia had to grab Edgar Lily out of school to help her.
'How can he be at school at a time like this?' Amelia sang down the hall to Susan Strange before careering down in the lift with her bicycle. She tightened the strap of her bright-yellow-crash-hat. The sleet flew down in vertical sheets. It would have been Amelia's last day of school term. Christmas Eve. Amelia slung her bike beside the

railings of London's School for No-Good Children. Sergeant Pepper prowled through the sludge into the playground. Amelia wondered how she was going to get into school and get Edgar OUT without being, noticed
by the great turkey herself, Mrs. Chump. She ummed and ahhed for a moment, deciding that she would be brave and head in as herself.
Amelia. Amelia Firebrand. Wa-Whoom!
There was very little of her Mama's Grown-Up Repellant left. She walked up the corridors with Flimsy Gizzards' strange name in her mind again. She wondered again if she would ever find out who he was.
Dicky Bells the Christmas carol played through the tinny speakers in the corridor. Walking past a bent plastic Christmas tree someone had stuffed a crisp packet on instead of an angel. Amelia could feel the Earth's pulse beneath her feet. But there was another shudder in the school too. Something vibrating in the walls. She held on tight to
Sergeant Pepper's tail, her fingers quivering. She pressed her ear to the door of Classroom Seven, hearing a weird noise from inside. It

wasn't the sound of chalk on an old- fashioned board. It wasn't the sound of chairs on dusty floorboards. It wasn't even the sound of chickens clucking!
'WHHEEE-PLUNK!'
Amelia stared down at her shoes. The sparkles on her red trainers had lit up like a car bonnet in the sun. There was a bright light underneath the door beaming into the corridor – and movement! A clunking and banging made the floor shake. Amelia knelt on the dusty floor, a staple stuck in her kneecap and a sharp piece of grit lodged in her palm. What was in there? A strange something! Amelia squinted through the lock. Shadows flailed left and right. The movement stopped. Her eye strained to see something. Any sort of clue.
'What is that?' she whispered.
The great whirring started again. A violent judder threw Amelia backwards. She stumbled, moved back to the door and clasped the brass handle. It was greasy! She dared herself to turn it. Was it Edgar and her class in there? There was so much noise coming from inside, whatever was in there would not be able to hear her sneak in.

Click! She turned the doorknob. The door opened with a squeak. The light was bright. Goose bumps
prickled her skin as she shielded her eyes. Amelia shook herself, turning her head back into the corridor. The incessant drip of an old radiator pipe. The cold concrete of the floor. A broken window filled with a cloudy sky. 'London's School for No-Good Children?' she asked.

The whirring and clunking was getting faster and the light was getting brighter. The door fell open.

WHIRRRR!CLoNK!WHIRRRR!CLoNK!WHIRR R!CLoNK! Amelia stared.

And she stared.

And she stared.

A squeak behind her made her jump. Edgar Lily! 'Edgar, what's going on? So much has happened. Are you OK?'

He grinned and pushed the door further open so Amelia could see better. The entire classroom was a buzz of activity. Every one of Amelia's classmates leapt around the room. Wild as monkeys. Their shirts skew-whiff. Their school ties knotted round their foreheads. They cheered at the spectacle in the middle of the room.

Mrs. Chump sat on a bicycle in her beige Crimplene trousers. The bicycle was powering an enormous contraption. She was shrieking up at the ceiling.

'YAHAHAHAHAHA! It's working! It's WOR-KING!' Her hair looked as though she had been dipped in glue and dried upside down. She was wild with passion and energy.

Amelia rubbed her eyes. There was only half a roof… the rest was SKY.

The contraption was as large as a double-decker bus.

Mrs. Chump's skinny bottom rocked to and fro as she pedaled.

'Well, I never have seen anything, if I haven't seen that.' Amelia closed her mouth. Edgar rolled in beside her, sweeping his white fringe from his brow. 'What d'ya reckon. We've been pretty busy.'

Amelia gave him a big kiss on the cheek, sending him scarlet red.

'You made this? It's Fantastic!' she said.
'What does it do?'

The creation heaved and pulled. Crafted of wooden junk – here a rocking chair, there a telegraph pole. Lifts and pulleys. Cogs and wheels turned to power four billowing sails.
'IT'S WORKING!' Mrs. Chump's bottom bounced higher.
Amelia heard the swarms of Uglies bobbing and buzzing happily up the corridor to join her. There was something really different and for a moment she didn't click as to what it was. She shaded her eyes from the bright sunshine in the classroom.
'Sunshine? That's it. How is there sun?'
She turned to Edgar Lily. He winked and pointed up at the top of the contraption. His pink eyes met her green eyes, their pupils tiny pinpricks in the light. Huge billowing sails whirred from a tall rotating mast, along with a huge Union Jack flag. Amelia grinned and realised what the machine was doing. It was clearing the clouds to allow sunshine back down and through to London! The sails whirred out like a windmill into the sky, whacking the clouds away far into the distance.
Wa-WOMB! The Earth's heartbeat.

Great beams of brilliant sunlight shone over the little patch of London that was London's School for
No-Good Children for the first time in years. The feeling in the classroom was one of joy. Each of Amelia's classmates whooped and yelped at their invention. She gawked at their skin. Their flesh was returning to blacks, pinks and browns.

With her Fantastic eyes she saw their Fantastic selves and rivers of delight flowed through her. Even Mrs. Chump was glowing with a radiant light. Her pinched and puckered nastiness transformed into wild sunlit delight.

'Amelia!' they cried when they saw her. 'Check this out!'

Mrs. Chump motioned with her hand. 'Let me introduce you to… The Great Cloud Batter, our Darling, Amelia Firebrand.'

The Uglies hummed with pleasure, swarming around Amelia. To her delight, the Fantastic Telly stood on a desk at the end of the classroom. She looked at Edgar and smiled. She mouthed the words, thank you, to him and marveled at how only SEVEN days ago, her life

had seemed so dull, so melancholy, so lacking in anything exciting. And here she was, her classmates
wild and free. Mrs. Chump…less N for Normal than EVER!
The bell rang and the pupils streamed out of the school yard into the yellow sludge, which now danced with the light of the winter sun. Gramps and the Love Machine waited for Amelia at the school gates. The Love Machine stood guard on two orange feet, shivering and gallumping down pieces of litter that whipped by in the wind. Out of its funnel, cascades of fresh leaves and petals billowed behind it. Gramps wore a green leotard over his comfortable day trousers.
'Looking good, Gramps!'
'You're damn right, Sister!'
Amelia leant the Fantastic Telly next to the Love Machine and got down on her hands and knees in the defrosting ice.
'I just want to check something,' she said looking at the warm sunshine melting the sludge on the surrounding pavements.
She listened to London's heartbeat.
Wa-WHOOM

Wa-WHOOM

Wa-WHOOM.

Amelia grinned.

The Earth kicked with a faster pulse. She felt a warmth surge through the concrete and into her hands.

'Are you getting better?' she asked it.

Wa-Womb. Wa-Womb. Wa-Womb.

YES.

'So that's it,' Amelia said. 'The more Wonder the children have, the more happy all the kids AND the Earth will be.'

'Ok. The plan is to take all this to Trafalgar Square. Tomorrow is Christmas Day. At three o'clock in the afternoon, London will face its most boring moment of the year. Londoners will have eaten all their Christmas turkey. Every household in England will be practically snoring! The Queen of England's speech will be broadcast on the television and every child and grown-up in London will have...' Amelia paused and took a deep breath... 'the Wonder sucked from their hearts and brains!'

Amelia grinned at Edgar Lily. Beneath her the pavement rippled and purred. She hopped from one foot to the other not knowing whether to laugh or cry.

'Edgar, what did you do to your chair?'

'I looked in the Fantastic Telly, Amelia! I found my Fantastic Self for SURE.'

His motorised wheelchair was painted with blazing red and yellow flames down the side. Edgar puffed his chest out.

'I got go-faster-stripes!' He spun his chair round and did a wheelie, skidding on the ice. 'I always knew that when I didn't see you turn into a clucking chicken that day, it was 'cos you were magic, Edgar Lily!' she said.

Amelia looked on in awe. 'Hold on to how you feel right now – it's amazing, right?' she said. 'Do you reckon a Wonder Crusher could touch any of us if we were all feeling this bloomin' FANTASTIC?'

'No! It could not!' Edgar Lily said, flexing his muscles. 'I reckon the way I feel right now, might actually be the best I can ever remember.'

Amelia watched him as he stared round at Pudding Bag Lane; his eyes goggled with all that he saw with his Fantastic eyes. 'It all looks SO beautiful! Who could have known?'

Amelia knelt down in the snow and they both stared out down the road they had known all their lives. The gentle sunlight warmed the passersby, their faces spreading with warm smiles.

Amelia reached into an iron gate which surrounded a skinny tree. She caressed the Earth that surrounded its roots with the soft of her hand.

'We're listening,' she whispered to the Earth. 'We're all here now. All your children.'

Christmas Day

AMELIA FIREBRAND DAY

Chapter 17

The Final Countdown

Amelia laid awake right through the early hours into Christmas Day. But not to see what Father Christmas had brought. She twiddled with her fingernails. She didn't know what would happen in the morning. She had no idea if London's children would know what to do. She had to trust that the Uglies had been spreading the word throughout the night. She woke up on Christmas day with the exhausted Uglies swarming over her bed back and forth to wake her up. A stuffed stocking did lie at the end of her bed. She scrambled up to feel what was inside. A Satsuma, an apple, a bag of chocolate bells. She threw them up in the air for the Uglies, who yapped and snapped with delight to munch them. The Uglies helped her dress, pulling out odd socks, holey jumpers and last year's trousers for her, which she pulled on all together. Gramps took one look at her and grinned.

'Whatever they say about you, 'Melia, it won't be that you were boring!'

She stood on tiptoe on the skirting board and looked across London. Wa-Womb. Her feet tingled.

Amelia reached into her school satchel and pulled out a handful of pencil crayons.

Mrs Chump wasn't here to see this time.

Amelia stood on tippy-toe and coloured-in the view of London again. She smeared huge great rays of sunshine light over the chimneypots. She drew huge forks of golden lightning. She drew great waves of brown Earth erupting from the pavements full of coloured seeds that burst with greens, reds, pinks and purples.

She looked on with a big grin on her face.

Amelia wet her finger and in the thin film of grime on her window pane wrote.

When This You See, Remember Me.

She looked down at the dirt on her fingertip.

It was time to go.

The London Underground's tube would be shut and it was a long walk to Trafalgar Square. Maybe three hours. The Uglies swarmed to hoist the Fantastic Telly up and out into the lift while Amelia made the final plans with Gramps.

'You get your Fantastic Self up on to the roof of Chewing Gum Gutters for three o'clock. When The Queen's speech begins and London starts to sleep, start the Great Cloud Batter whirring. Gramps,' she said. 'I won't mess this up, will I?'

'If you do, then we'll mess it up together,' Gramps said with a gappy grin, tinkering with the mechanism in the Love Machine and wiping sweat from his brow.

It was the longest day of Amelia's life EVER. Her feet ached. Trafalgar Square stood huge and empty in the city centre. Its enormous stone fountains and flocks of pigeons looked strange without the usual thousands of tourists taking photos and buying bird-seed.

It was six minutes past three o'clock in Trafalgar Square. Its enormous Christmas tree bowed in the cold wind sweeping the square. Amelia drummed her fingers on the stone edge of a water fountain.

'Why isn't it working? Where is everyone?' She peered up each of the empty streets. Fading Christmas lights swayed in the ice cold wind. Amelia unrolled the TV Fun magazine and checked the programme times. She had definitely got it right. Christmas Day, 3pm the Queen's Speech.

But where was everyone? She knelt down on to the pavement. She couldn't feel the Earth's pulse at all.

No, Wa-Whoom?

Amelia's jaw tightened.

The power of this Wonder Crusher was beyond anything she could comprehend.

Silence. Spooky eerie city silence.

A chilling screech, like fingernails down a chalkboard made her jump up.

Amelia turned in horror and watched the stone head of every statue in Trafalgar Square drooping downwards to their chest.

A deep snore started to whisper from their plinths.

Amelia shivered.

So, this was it. This is the Brain Drain. This is ALL of the Wonder being Crushed.

Suddenly Amelia Firebrand loved London and EVERYONE in it more than anything.

London was falling asleep. She had to wake it up!

She pulled her daffodil-yellow anorak tight and buckled her bright-yellow-crash-hat tight, squeezing her chin. She had to stay awake too.

Amelia closed her eyes and dropped into her heart and asked to see what was happening across London. Clear as day she was shown. Like a shadow at dusk, the Brain Drain moved across London. Buildings creaked old and tired, windows yawned, door shutters rolled down, households slowed. Mums and Dads, Grandmas and Grandpas went for a lie down. Children rolled to sleep in front of the Queen's Speech. Parents' eyelids drooped. London and its people were dying.

Amelia yelled, leaping her arms in the air into Trafalgar Square.

'Wake Up, London!'

She spun round in horror. Pigeons tucked their head beneath their wings on the spot. A huge churning mass of black clouds appeared in the sky. Cobwebs spun themselves and draped across every building. Traffic lights stopped chatting to one another, their tops wilting. Amelia felt the sleep coming. As though the dark sky were singing her a sinister lullaby, she stumbled woozy into a bin. She swooned and sighed. The sun sunk low in the sky. The moon appeared in the east and winked.

Amelia shook her head. What on Earth was she doing? She couldn't fall asleep too. She stood up, shook herself down and marched back and forth on the spot.

Around her, electric cables and pipes were shooting through the paving slabs, coiling up and round bins, lampposts, traffic lights. She recalled every Fantastic moment she could remember in the last few days to stay awake - Blue and pink feathered chicks, the Love Machine, Gramps and Amelia eating a meal together, finding the Fantastic telly!

But oh, how woozy and blissful it would be to sleep. How nice, how easy, how... NO.

She walked around the empty streets, deciding that the only way to make this happen was if she herself, Amelia Firebrand found her way back into the Wonder Crusher. First she would have to stop the Prime Monster from being able to stop her.

Walking past the Horse Guards she saw that even the Queen of

England's soldiers in their black fur hats had fallen asleep at their posts. Their hat straps lost in the folds beneath their chins. She stopped at the end of Number Ten Downing Street and peered down to the sleeping guard at its door. How would she know if the Prime Monster was in there or not?

She decided that she couldn't know. Not without the Earth guiding her.

She pulled out the bottle of her Mama's Flimsy Gizzard's Grown-Up Repellent and tugged the cork out. She peered down into the bottle, pressing her eye to its cold rim.

A swirl of liquid no deeper than the width of her fingertip had pooled at the bottom. Hardly any left at all.

Amelia gulped down her fear.

'And all of London being turned to sleeping stones - what if I can't do anything about it?' She tugged at her gold streak pulling it into curly spikes out the front of her crash-hat.

She had to stop the Prime Monster from being able to get to her. She smeared a finger's worth of repellent around Number Ten's door frame. That would keep him locked inside for sure. Then she turned and headed for Westminster.

Snoring benches languished with snoozing traffic lights. Amelia concentrated hard not to fall asleep. Thick concrete crept up the city bench legs.

Amelia's legs weakened at the knees. The city was folding in on itself.

Big Ben wilted like a daisy stalk. The hands of its clock dangling into the river.

Amelia saw that the doors to the Houses of Parliament were sealing together. She ran to the doors watching the seal mould its way around the frame and up from by her feet up the crack. She slipped her

fingers in-between the two doors and prised them open, sliding one foot into the hall and slipping the other in quick behind it. The door sealed with a squeak.

She was in!

Amelia turned and gawped. A hush filled the cavernous entrance hall. But a strong vibration in the wooden floors signalled to her that the Wonder Crusher was at full power. The green velvet panelling click-clacked together jig sawing up and over the windows.

Yawning gargoyles shuddered disappearing into the alcoves. Amelia took small steps through the hall. Each footstep echoed with a clonk up the walls. And when she reached the great room where all the debating Monsters of Parliament had been working themselves up, she found that the green carpeting had crept up over the benches and over the door in the wooden paneling. How would she get through to the Wonder Crusher?

The floor vibrated and shook. Amelia fought with the crawling carpet to pull it down, revealing the oak paneled door. She yanked it open and scrabbled into the back room. The door swung closed behind

her. She was doubly trapped now. How would she ever escape? Maybe this was it. She would die alone in the Houses of Parliament. But her worries were forgotten when she heard the sound of the Wonder Crusher. It barfed and belched churning and writhing at full power. Amelia saw a grid of lights on the wall, all marking each household in London that was draining of Wonder with incessant flashes. A large siren on top of the Wonder Crusher turned, lighting her face.

The Wonder Crusher looked full to burst. Out the other end reams of banknotes streamed into plastic pallets. Millions and billions and trillions of pounds were firing themselves to the ceiling casting a dark shadow over Amelia. She took one last look, glared at the Wonder Crusher, and decided to STOP this all once and for all.

She knew she had to remove her bright-yellow-crash-hat. Her life seemed to stop as she unbuckled its strap and placed it on the ground. She was going to go in. And she might not survive.

She rolled up her sleeves, took a deep breath and clambered up on to
the highest edge of the Wonder Crusher.

She opened the top hatch. A kaleidoscopic scream of stolen Wonder roared from its depth. A whirl of darkening lights...

Amelia Firebrand THREW herself in to the Wonder Crusher.

It chundered and choked in response. Amelia squeezed her whole face shut and waded down head first, pulling herself with her arms, swimming into the vat of psychedelic custard.

Feeling like an astronaut in space, her arms and legs could barely move.

She reached the bottom and her hands and feet flailed as she reached for every cable, plug, bolt she could, yanking them from their holds. Her flesh and bones were whacked and battered by the cogs and wheels and churning machine parts deep in the custardy-goo of London's Wonder. With her last breath in her lungs she wailed.

'I've had enough of you!' she screamed in the goo. Choking and spluttering.

'You're awful and horrid and I say NO to it ALL.' She inhaled a deep lungful of the jellied mass. Every muscle
of her face was contorted with defiance. She heaved and hauled at it still, going purple with exhaustion, kicking and spitting with every ounce of loving rage she had. She was desperate for breath. She turned and swam back to the surface.

Amelia emerged and hauled herself out on to the side of the vat.

'STOP RIGHT THERE!' a voice boomed from the arches.

Amelia froze and swung her head to look up out of the machinery.

The Prime Monster, Sebastian Peach stood, hands on hips in full regalia. He wore a purple suit with a golden crown on his head at a jaunty angle.

'You wally!' Amelia shouted. 'You can't do this to London's children!' Amelia clambered out drenched with oozing fluorescent goo. She slid down the steps and faced him head-on.

'We're only little! And we're full of magic and ideas and good stuff. You can't put us in rows and suck out our Wonder out. IT'S OURS! We were born with it. Give it back!'

'Police!' The Prime Monster called out. 'Arrest this maggot!' He scooped a deposit from his nostril and smeared it on the Wonder Crusher. He pulled out the TARGET photograph of her from his left lapel and sneered at it.

'So, it IS you. You little worm! What do you know about WONDER?' he barked. 'For me, the Wonder IS power and money in bank accounts stuffed with diamonds, bombs and weapons. Your Wonder is for teddy bears and dollies and you don't need it!'

Seven police officers appeared with hypnotic twirling red and white lights in their eyes. Amelia closed her eyes. She focused and felt the Earth beneath her feet.

She felt the Earth's love in every cell of her body. She felt the Earth that created every bone in her body and every hair on her fuzzy head.

She didn't have her Mama, but she WAS still a child of the earth and the Universe, she realised.

In her inner vision flashed a picture of the Prime Monster – as a BOY.

'But you were a boy once too! You must remember, you must! Days were meant to feel good. Someone's taken your joy TOO!'

The police grabbed Amelia and dragged her backwards.

Amelia kicked and screamed, her face turned purple. She saw the Prime Minister throw the target photograph on the ground with disgust.

Deep inside Amelia Firebrand heard a voice.

CALL ME. Mama? CALL ME. Mama?

I'll help you, 'Melia. Just call. 'MAMA!'

Amelia screamed.

The windows smashed into smithereens from the pitch. 'I LOVE YOU!' Wa-Womb.

A new sound burst from The Wonder Crusher. It crunched and cracked behind her. The police dropped Amelia and swung round with their batons.

'You goons, don't let go of her!' the Prime Monster barked.

Amelia turned and stared.

The Wonder Crusher's belly bulged. It looked about to burst. The psychedelic custard of Wonder swelled and ballooned up and mushroomed out of the vat.

The Prime Monster yelped and grabbed hold of a low hanging chandelier. Amelia pulled herself up a pillar quick smart. The police shrieked. The Wonder engulfed them in a dazzling beam of brilliant lights.

'Arrrrghhhhhh!' The Prime Monster screamed, his peachy bottom doing a jig in the air.

Amelia took her chance. She unbuckled her bright-yellow-crashhat and hurled it right at the bull's-eye on his buttocks.

Score!

He fell with a gigantic plop into the Wonder. His shrieks echoed in the arches. The Wonder reached the edges of the room and settled into a giant trifle. Amelia gently lowered herself onto its surface and hopped across to the Wonder Crusher.

The Wonder Crusher ground to a halt with an enormous shudder. Then a slow gentle whirr began from within the machine. And with a little squeak with its remaining energy, a reel of freshly pressed twenty pound notes bearing Amelia Firebrand's grinning portrait appeared. She gawped and peeled a few notes up to show Gramps and

turned to leave, picking up her bright-yellow-crash-hat.

Behind her, she saw emerging from the Wonder custard, eight small wet and disheveled boys in old fashioned school uniforms – the police officers and the Prime Monster – the Wonder had given them back their Wonder. They were little boys again. Behind them, the Wonder from the Wonder Crusher burst up through the glass domed roof. Huge fountains of coloured brights spumed up and into the City of London.

Amelia whooped and buckled her bright-yellow-crash-hat on tight beneath her chin. Jumping

over the target photograph the Prime Monster had dropped; Amelia grabbed it and stuffed it into her pocket. She was no-one's target!
She tore off her sparkly-red trainers and threw her socks over towards a bin, and ran and ran and ran as fast she could, yelling down the streets. The soft soles of her feet pound the pavement. She spun round, throwing her arms in the air.
'WAKE UP, LONDON!!!!' Amelia yelled with delight. Wa-Womb!
The Earth boomed beneath her.
The ground shuddered. She balanced to stay upright. Around her, red post boxes, lampposts and telephone boxes trembled.
A loud CRACK! LIGHT EVERYWHERE BEAMED!
Amelia gawped as tons of deep warm brown Earth pushed its way up and through the gutters, manhole covers and drains with volcanic warmth.
A bolt of golden lightning split the sky. Showers of starlight sprayed down to London. Amelia danced around and around, leaping into the air.
The Houses of Parliament rocketed open with plumes of light; the children's Wonder free to

soar. Flumes of fireworking, Catherinewheeling DELIGHT and JOY and COLOUR lit the cloudy sky. As the Wonder returned to London, thousands of London's children swarmed from every flat, terrace, row and street. They tore of their shoes. They ripped of their socks.

Wa-Whoom!

Wa-Whoom!

Wa-Whoom!

They scooted, roller skated, ran and ran and ran through the city to reach Trafalgar Square, where they

swarmed in from the adjoining roads, Whitehall and Regent Street.

In her wildest dreams, Amelia could not have imagined a more beautiful sight.

From up ahead she could see Gramps, he had harnessed himself to Nelson' Column and was waving a huge Union Jack but painted all the colours of the rainbow for all people and a sparkling flash of red glitter paint.

Just like her trainers!

Amelia's arms reached high above her head. The Uglies dangled her over the Fantastic Telly on an enormous stone plinth, without a statue on it. The Telly landed and the whole square thundered with a cheer. Amelia shook with a bolt of adrenalin. She steadied herself on the plinth and looked into the eyes of a sea of unfathomably excited faces. Thousands of children's hands waved at her. Amelia took a deep breath and picked up her megaphone with her tiny hands.

'The Wonder Crusher is gone. Climb up and see your Fantastic selves and we'll make our London
FANTASTIC! The grown-ups don't know how to do it - we have to do it!!!'

The children clambered up the plinth. The Uglies hummed and buzzed to each child giving them a hand, a nose or a knee up. Amelia and Gramps reached down to haul more up one by one. Vines and flowers furled up and around the telly around the plinths. Some children stood for a few seconds in front of their reflection. Others took longer. It's as though they are seeing what they already knew could be true, Amelia thought to herself. One boy gawped and gawped. His hands pressed to the Fantastic
Telly, his mouth hanging open. Amelia watched with fascination. Each child saw and

remembered their most Fantastic selves. Kids leapt down from the plinth one by one into their new world.

A boy with ginger hair goggled up at the sky. 'I can hear the clouds creaking to rain!'

Amelia saw a small girl with pigtails pressing her ear to the paving slabs. 'London's got a heartbeat!' she said, her eyes wide.

Amelia peered over the crowds to see children running around exploring their new London down side streets. She saw them listening to walls – hearing the ancient bricks' stories. She saw that the gargoyles perching along the gutters jabbered away with the pigeons that nestled on them. She saw the Fantastic children start doing mad things. Things that were wild and wonderful.

They sowed grass and wild flower seeds along the roads between the cracks. On top of phone boxes. On mini-roundabouts. Inside postboxes. They listened to the paths where millions of people had trodden and felt the sadness of the grown-ups for hundreds of years.

The children's hearts bloomed with love for the grown-ups. They looked around at the grey world the adults had created and knew they could change it. Wee-stained corners bloomed with the trees and flowers children were planting.

Amelia's heart soared, watching the Wonder pushing through the cracks in the pavement, up and into London. She turned to see coffee shops coughing out their paper cups. Office windows spewed out

years of boring documents. Photocopiers flung themselves to death down several floors. The Love Machine galumphed around munching up all of the useless gumpf! The transformed gumpf spouted from its funnel as a huge flume of feathers, seaweeds, shells and trailing vines. LIGHT SHINED THROUGH EVERYTHING!

Lush green blades of grass and skinny weedy weeds jostled for space, each one swelled and filled the streets in minutes. Sweet honeysuckle blooms trailed up every wall. Postboxes erupted with pollen-filled buds. Traffic cones buzzed with bumble bees. Amelia got down on her hands and knees and listened for London' heartbeat.

There it was.

Wa-Womb!

Wa-Womb!

Wa-WOMB!

The Earth's heartbeat.

'She's ALIVE!' Amelia said.

The Earth's pulse was strong. Without love and wonder, nothing could survive, Amelia realised. Just like her.

And N for Normal wasn't as delightful as F for blooming

Fantastic!

Across the square, she heard a shrieking whistle being blown, and turned to see the flash of blue lights. A rabble of fresh police officers bolted out on to the fresh green grass of Trafalgar Square. They bumbled into one another. A police car skidded into a laughing lamppost.

'Here, what's going on?' they yelled, speaking into their walkietalkies and shaking their batons at the children. To Amelia's delight the Fantastic children jumped up and down around the officers, draping them in garlands and dousing them in steaming custard and fruity jam. An officer shot up into the air with surprise. He grabbed the laughing lamppost.

A few of the policemen seemed to be waking up too. They looked at the weapons tied to their bodies. She saw them looking confused. Amelia laughed till her sides ached and some pee came out in her pants, watching some of them wiggle out of their uniforms. They stood in their faded white underdungers, jumped into the fountains and started splashing around. Some flung their batons, guns, tazers and handcuffs on to the ground. The Love Machine jolted over on his big orange feet. Munch, munch, munch! Their weapons spewed out and down the inflatable slide of the Love Machine as bright love bubbles, which drifted up and over the square, popping on everyone's heads.
'There she is!' Amelia heard a purple officer cry. 'SHE'S THE ONE! Arrest her, at once!'
A stream of hundreds of children charged towards Amelia Firebrand lifting her up on to their heads, passing her from safe arms to even safer arms far away from the police. They danced on cars and whooped and cheered. Amelia laughed. She felt safe! She felt secure in the wild chaos of the Fantastic children. She felt no more fear. Amelia Firebrand unstrapped her crash-hat and threw it into the crowd of

Fantastic children and fluorescent bright pigeons flocking around them.

Wa-Whoom! The Earth's heartbeat.

From somewhere in the crowds, the bearded nature presenter appeared – 'And here, we have the sweaty English basin of London City. And this, a Little Girl,' he said twiddling his matted beard.

'A Little Girl who has just stumbled into a cosmic and ancient long-forgotten Secret. A secret so beautiful that all of London will breathe again, and all of London will laugh again and all of London will be free to play again, as they had always dreamed in their hearts that they could.'

Chapter 18

Golden Light

It was quiet in the sitting room. The first quiet Amelia Firebrand had had since the morning, eight days ago that she had knelt down on to the pavement outside London's School for No-Good Children and heard the secrets of the earth and all the Universe. The Uglies snored and tooted the odd honk from their scatterings round the room. Gramps snored in the corner.
Amelia stood a drawing she had made of a heart on the Fantastic Television, amidst its coils of flowers and leaves. She kneeled down in front of it.
Are you there, telly? I'm here if you want to talk, she said. I want to talk to you.
The telly's air vents fizzed with a blue light and the familiar smell of it heating up filled

Amelia's nostrils. She quivered and pressed her palm to the screen.

'Hi,' she whispered.

The Fantastic screen lit up.

'So, Amelia Firebrand' it whispered in a crackling hiss. 'Together at last.'

It was the calmest moment in days and the most exciting.

Amelia turned to look at everyone snoozing. Even Sergeant Pepper, the chick and the rabbit snoozed happily in the magazine rack.

Amelia knew what she wanted to ask the telly. She had two questions.

'Let me see myself. I want to see. I won't pass out this time. I

P for Promise.' Easy,' the telly said. The screen fizzed with light. She leant in closer. Amelia Firebrand's face lit up.

Her fuzz of brown hair, her chocolate dark skin, her emerald green eyes, her grey school jumper radiated with a light. The light shone from her heart and filled the room with her very own luminescent glow. Not at all scary like the first time she had seen herself. The light was dazzling.

I am my most Fantastic Self, she said.

'A is for Amelia,' said the Fantastic Telly.

'F is for Fantastically Firebrand,' she grinned.

Her fingertips touched the reflection.

'Please,' she said smiling, 'I want to see, well, I don't quite know what I mean, but, I want to see what you are? What is it that is speaking to me and sending me magic and text messages and chicks with tickets? And filling my life with so much magic that I am forever changed.' What is this Fantastic Borderland of Things?

The telly reflection seemed to smile and swirled with the familiar warmth of its golden handwriting.

'We would show you, but we wouldn't want to scare you,' the words said kindly.

'Me, scared?' Amelia whispered, her mind racing with the zillions of mad moments in the last few days. 'I'm not that scaredy-a-cat.'

'We've seen you hiding under your covers at night,' the telly's screen turned up at the edges to smile.

'Pleeeeeasssse!' Amelia said. 'I can see everything else!

Everything. Show me what you are. I promise I won't run away.'

'All right, dear heart. Because it is your wish. But, we are not a thing, we are instead, what makes up everything.'

Every cell in Amelia's body lit up. Around her, the room lit with billions of what looked like crystalline light particles brilliant in the dark. Everything was alive. Everything was light.

Amelia swooshed her hand through the light. All of life was ALIVE. Every breath, every dust, every bit of dirt, everything.

And she knew that she could touch it all. With her love, her heart.

'Can I really touch you all?' she asked. And in her heart she had a sudden thought of Sergeant Pepper and she felt more love.

The golden crystalline light heard her from within and millions of light particles streamed before her eyes and in the air before her, the light formed into the shape of a cat in the air with a poomf it then vanished into the light.

'Dolphin!' Amelia Firebrand whispered.

The golden lights parted and remerged, a diving dolphin swimming before her eyes.

'Is it what I see in my heart that I see in the world?,' Amelia grinned.

She concentrated hard on a chair in the corner of the room, beaten up and tired. She asked it to lift up. It did. It fell to the carpet with a thud. She glared at it with her darkest feeling of dread, anger and sadness.

The chair immediately festered into rotting mulch.

She took a few deep breaths and found the love in her again and gazed at the chair.

The chair grew the softest wings and the fine pink tapestry rewove itself back together.

Amelia raised her hand and the objects in the room lifted, she lowered her hand and the objects collapsed to the floor.

She closed her eyes and asked for the room to be as it wanted to be in accordance with her most natural Fantastic Self.

The room whirlpooled into lights. Every object lifted and spun in a whirling vortex of patterns and shapes around her. Amelia clapped and jumped and danced and sang. The orange, pink, blue and yellow chicks peeped and

chirped in the whirlpool with delight. Amelia marvelled at the WONDER of it all, her heart bursting with love.
She ducked underneath it all and pulled out a notepad from her bedside table. The rabbit clucked
quietly, being lifted up in the swirling softness. Amelia wrote a title on the notepad cover...

How to be a Human Being
(...not one brought up by chickens)
by Amelia Firebrand age 10 ¾

Amelia stood holding her notebook in her hand and looked up through the window to the full moon shining bright above the city. It had never looked more serenely beautiful. She shot a rocket of love up to it with a rush of love and gratitude for her Mama and all her new love and wonder. This magic is real, REAL. And it could make sad people happy and it could make broken things fixed and it could make an ugly thing beautiful and, and, and, Amelia's head raced with all the magical everythings.

Her breath was quick and through her school jumper, her heart beat strong and sure.
This was just the B for
Beginning.

Amelia Firebrand never knew how alone she felt until the day the Earth and the entire Universe started speaking to her. Up until then she was completely normal. A little bit bored. A little bit lonely. But apart from that, for a ten-and-three-quarter-year old girl, completely Normal.
She had hands that were good for picking things up and legs that were very good for walking. She was as small as a button, well not quite. And she had an afro of brown curls, with a streak of gold along one side of her head. Honey warm skin, and deep soulful eyes. It was what was inside Amelia that made her different. Like you, she had a soul. What she hadn't known was that her soul was a magic one and it was as old as the Earth.
She knew now.
Amelia felt her feet firmly on the ground.
Wa-Whoom. There it was.
Wa-Womb.

There it was again. A slow, rhythmic thud.
A heartbeat. The ground beneath London was ALIVE.
And all of London was turning completely fruity. She looked up and out of the window to the stars above London, the Universe of love that surrounded her. The LIGHT that was awake and alive in all things.
For the first time Amelia Firebrand felt N for Normal, not because she had run away. Not because she had hidden.
But because she AND everyone else was now Absolutely, Utterly, Bananas, Crackers, Wondrous,
Magical and utterly Fantastic.
That's with a capital F.
"*****************'' Amelia sang with a big grin on her face.
Amelia pressed her palm to her heart.
As she leant forwards to clutch her notebook, the Prime Monster's target photograph fell from her pocket and on to the carpet.
Amelia picked it up. And stared. Wa-Whoom.
It was an old faded photograph of a young man with an ice-cream cone curl of yellow hair. He was sat on a bench wearing brown trousers.

'Sebastian Peach,' Amelia whispered.

The photo was ripped down the middle.

Half of it was missing.

In his arms, the young man in the photo held a baby girl. She had skin as soft as honey, and soulful brown eyes, a button nose and frizzy curls.

Amelia reached into her satchel for the photograph of her Mama sitting on the bench, and pieced the two halves together.

They fit.

She touched the streak of gold in her hair.

'Papa?' Amelia gasped, clutching her chest.

Wa-Womb! Her whole being beat with the Earth.

And, Amelia Firebrand realised... ...that this was just the B for Beginning.

Acknowledgements

to those that know who they are,
who I need not name.
Those that have enriched my every waking moment, teaching me to become a human being (and to find my fantastic self) and trust a Divine in it all. Thankyou.

Beloveds, family and friends those that I have loved and laughed with and whom without I would never have grown and life could not be the same. Thank you.
The Journey Never Ends.

No matter what your story or where you are at on your life soul path…
Remember you are loved by something beautiful something so bright so loving something bigger than you a Divine Light in All Things x
And So It Is.

In love.

Your friend, phoenix x

Printed in Great Britain
by Amazon